Water Wise

Safety for the Recreational Boater

By Jerry Dzugan and Susan Clark Jensen

The following Sea Grant Programs enthusiastically recommend use of this book in their states:

Alaska Sea Grant

California Sea Grant College System

Connecticut Sea Grant College Program

Florida Sea Grant

Illinois-Indiana Sea Grant College Program

Maine-New Hampshire Sea Grant

Maryland Sea Grant

Mississippi-Alabama Sea Grant

New York Sea Grant

North Carolina Sea Grant College Program

Pennsylvania Sea Grant

Oregon Sea Grant

Texas Sea Grant College Program

University of Southern California Sea Grant Program

University of Wisconsin Sea Grant Institute

Washington Sea Grant Program

WHOI Sea Grant (Woods Hole Oceanographic Institution)

Published by University of Alaska Sea Grant and U.S. Marine Safety Association

Elmer E. Rasmuson Library Cataloging-in-Publication Data

Dzugan, Jerry.

        Water wise : safety for the recreational boater / by Jerry Dzugan and Susan Clark Jensen.

(MAB-51)

1. Boats and boating—Safety measures. 2. Survival skills. 3. Aquatic sports. I. Jensen, Susan Clark.

II. Title. III. Series: Marine advisory bulletin ; no. 51.

GV777.55.D98 1999

ISBN 1-56612-058-6

Marine Advisory Bulletin 51

The Publishers

The **University of Alaska Sea Grant College Program** is cooperatively supported by the U.S. Department of Commerce, NOAA Office of Sea Grant, under grant no. NA86RG0050, project A/75-01; and by the University of Alaska with state funds. The University of Alaska is an affirmative action/equal opportunity employer and educational institution.

    Sea Grant is a unique partnership with public and private sectors combining research, education, and technology transfer for public service. This national network of universities meets changing environmental and economic needs of people in our coastal, ocean, and Great Lakes Regions.

    The **United States Marine Safety Association** (USMSA) is an organization of manufacturers, service corporations, sale representatives, and individuals involved in products or services that promote safety at sea. The mission of the USMSA is to be the recognized world leader in the marine safety and survival industry; to promote the development and implementation of the highest possible performance, manufacturing, maintenance, service and training standards, for all lifesaving, survival and emergency rescue equipment; to be a centralized network for the collection and dissemination of useful information; and to serve and educate the membership, the general public, and governing agencies in a manner which exhibits a commitment to the highest degree of quality and integrity.

Published by

University of Alaska Sea Grant	and	U.S. Marine Safety Association
P.O. Box 755040		1900 Arch St.
Fairbanks, Alaska 99775-5040		Philadelphia, Pennsylvania 19103-1498
(907) 474-6707		(215) 564-3484
http://www.uaf.alaska.edu/seagrant		

Table of Contents

Acknowledgments

The authors thank Charlene Hoppe and the Board of Directors of the U.S. Marine Safety Association who sponsored and made this publication a reality. Greg Switlik, Switlik Parachute Company, is to be thanked for his initial proposal of this project and his encouragement.

Many people helped immensely by contributing material, answering questions, and reviewing various drafts of this manuscript. It is a better product because of their help: Marian Allen of AMSEA; Charlie Bond of Ralston, Cunningham & Associates; T.J. Duff of USCG; James Falk of Delaware Sea Grant; Dan Falvey of AMSEA; Kari Guddal of Imperial International, Inc.; Karen Hanson of USA Services; Sue Hargis of USCG 17th District; Paul Helland of Vessel Safety Corporation; Richard Hiscock of ERE Associates; Bob Haggarty of USCG; Jim Herbert of the Alaska Vocational Technical College; Dewayne Hollin of Texas Sea Grant; Charlene Hoppe of USMSA; Leslie Hughes of North Pacific Fishing Vessel Owners Association; Dug Jensen of the Educational Training Company; Karl Johnson of Haines, AK; John Malatak of USCG; Robert Markle of USCG; Matt Murphy of WoodenBoat Magazine; Matt Odum of USCG; Kathy O'Gara of the Southeast Alaska Regional Health Consortium; Susan Scott of Honolulu, HI; John Schwartz of Michigan Sea Grant Extension; Rick Steiner of University of Alaska Marine Advisory Program; Al Stevens of USCG; Steve Stewart of Michigan Sea Grant Extension; and Howard Wright of Port Supply. Beaver Sports, Fairbanks, Alaska, lent equipment and clothing for photographs.

A special thanks to the Alaska Marine Safety Education Association for its office, technical, and moral support, and to Sue Keller and the staff at Alaska Sea Grant for editing, graphics, layout, and printing.

Authors' note: Throughout the book male pronouns are used; they are intended to apply to both males and females.

About the Authors

Jerry Dzugan has been the director and training coordinator of the Alaska Marine Safety Education Association (AMSEA) since 1986. He has worked as a boating safety trainer since 1985, and has also been a commercial fisherman, charterboat operator, and emergency medical services instructor. Dzugan is an affiliate faculty member of the University of Alaska Southeast, and has earned safety awards from the Alaska Safety Advisory Council, National Safe Boating Council, National Safety Council, U.S. Department of Health and Human Services, and the U.S. Marine Safety Association. He makes his home and maintains his sailboat in Sitka, Alaska.

Susan Clark Jensen lives in Sitka, Alaska, where she trains safety instructors and teaches for AMSEA. Jensen was a founding board member of AMSEA, and has served as Emergency Medical Services coordinator for Southeast Alaska Regional Health Corporation and Southeast Region EMS Council. She is editor of *Beating the Odds on the North Pacific: A Guide to Fishing Safety*, published by University of Alaska Sea Grant, and is author of the *First Aid Book* published by the Southeast Alaska Regional Health Corporation.

Credits

Cover and book design by Dave Brenner, editing by Sue Keller, University of Alaska Sea Grant. Illustrations: p. 5 N. Van Veenen; p. 10 r., 33, 44, 54, 89, 90, 92 J. Schmitts; p. 16, 22, 40, 41l., 45, 47 S. Lawrie; p. 5bottom,10 l., 11, 12, 26, 27, 28, 31, 32, 38, 39top, 41r., 43, 58, 61, 62, 66, 68-71, 73, 76, 77, 80, 88(after Sherrodd), 93, 104-107, 116, 119l., 120l., 121, 122, 124, 130, 132, 133, 137, 139, 141, 146, 148, 163, 166, 170, 172, 173, 183 D. Brenner; p. 39 bottom V. Culp; p. 86 K. Sherrodd; p. 119r. K. Beebee; pp. 120r. K. Lundquist; p. 169 L. Sporleder after USCG. Front and back cover photographs by Dave Brenner.

Preface

Sailing or cruising in your boat should be an enjoyable and exhilarating experience. But, are you ready for the day when something goes really wrong? You may find yourself having to survive in cold and stormy conditions for an extended period, while you wait for help. You need to have the proper survival equipment, and know how to use it. Will the help come in hours or will you have to survive for days? Rescue will come sooner if you filed a float plan and if you have the right emergency communication and signaling equipment.

Prevention—avoiding threatening situations—is the most important thing you can do. *Water Wise* helps you prepare for a safe trip, practice safe seamanship, and recognize approaching danger. Preparedness—being ready to survive in the water with the proper equipment and the seven steps to survival—is the other part. *Water Wise* presents the information skippers and crew need to know in a very readable, direct way. Being equipped to the Coast Guard's minimum safety standards is just the start, especially for going offshore. Skippers need to understand their risks and responsibilities for their type of operation, and prepare accordingly.

Much has been learned from those who have survived for days and even weeks at sea. You can do it if you need to and if you are ready. *Water Wise* builds on the work done several years ago in *Beating the Odds in the North Pacific*, the definitive safety and survival guide for commercial fishermen working in some of the world's most hostile waters. Now, *Water Wise* will help recreational boaters to recognize and correct conditions that threaten their vessels and their lives.

Courtesy of Center for Great Lakes and Aquatic Sciences

A 42-year-old man borrowed a 20-foot dinghy from a friend for a trip from Pigeon Point to Mt. Irvine, Tobago. What should have been a five-mile, 30-minute boat ride ended up lasting **four days.** What happened? He ran out of gas and ended up drifting 117 miles in the Caribbean before being rescued by a Venezuelan fishing boat.

The morning after the engines quit he discovered that the boat was carrying $1^1/_2$ liters of water, a tarp, a leather engine cover, and a bucket. **He put everything to use,** crouching inside the leather cover much of the time for protection from the sun by day and the cold at night. He remarked, "When you get wet out there with the winds blowing, it's like coming onto the beach after a sea bath without a towel. Believe me, it's chilling."

Flying fish, seaweed, and rain water helped keep him alive, as did his will to live. "I had to set goals and keep hope," he said.

"Survival" by Alva Viarruel, Trinidad Express Features, May 22, 1997

B oating with your family and friends can be a relaxing experience on a beautiful day. But sometimes a carefree trip can end a bit differently than expected.

It's easy to get complacent and think, "The weather is nice...It's just a short trip that I've made many times with no problems..." But, in the words of one seasoned captain, "Just because you haven't had any problems, it doesn't mean you are being safe."

PREPARING FOR A SAFE TRIP

What do you need to think about before heading out? Here are six critical factors:

1. Your boat.

2. Who will be on board.

3. Where you are going.

4. The environment.

5. Your equipment.

6. What might go wrong with any of the above.

You don't want to be so paranoid that you can't untie from the dock, but a prudent mariner plans ahead, both to prevent problems (like making sure he has enough fuel!), and to think about what he will do when problems arise. And they will.

This book is intended to help you think about these six areas so you can be prepared for a fun, safe trip.

1. Your Boat

Know your boat's capabilities, both what it can and cannot do. Sometimes the best decision is **Don't!** Don't make that crossing right now. Don't bring those three extra people along even though they would be fun to have on board. It just isn't worth having an unstable vessel.

Boats are great, but they are things, and things can break. Think about what could go wrong: An engine that won't start, flooding that won't stop, and fire where it doesn't belong. Do you have any plans in case your nightmares come true? Chapter 12, Fire Fighting and Fire Prevention, and Chapter 13, Safe Seamanship, can help you get prepared.

2. Who Will Be On Board?

A trip with five adults would be a lot different from one with two adults and three preschoolers. (How's that for obvious?) But think for a moment how different the adult cruise would be if all five drank alcohol. Consider whether the people on board will be able to help you if anything goes wrong.

Will you allow alcohol on board? What will you do if someone falls overboard? What injuries or medical problems might occur and how many can you prevent? Simple things like using sunscreen, and having enough clothing, food, and water for your passengers plus extra for emergencies can prevent some problems.

3. Where You Are Going

File a float plan before you go. One of the main reasons stranded people get found is that someone misses them and starts looking for them.

Are there likely to be other boaters where you are headed? If not, be sure you have some way to communicate, and to stay warm and dry if you don't make it home or to your destination.

THE FAR SIDE   By Gary Larson

Your route, destination, and proximity to other boaters will help determine the equipment you bring.

4. The Environment

What's it like out there? Listen to the weather forecast, make your own weather observations, and **figure out how the tides and currents will affect your plans.** How hot or how cold is it likely to be? The environment will also impact your equipment and clothing choices. See Chapter 2, Reading the Weather.

5. Your Equipment

Equipment alone isn't going to save you, but it sure can help make your difficulties and disasters more tolerable. Get a copy of **Federal Requirements and Safety Tips for Recreational Boats** (see Resources, p. 176) for the latest word on what you are required to have on board. Remember, this booklet lists the **minimum** amount of equipment.

With so many different brands and models to consider, how do you decide what equipment to buy? Price, warranty, the company's reputation, ease of returns and servicing, and recommendations from others will influence your decisions. Some equipment will be marked SOLAS-approved. What does that mean?

SOLAS, or **Safety Of Life At Sea,** originated after the loss of the *Titanic,* when people realized that survival standards were inadequate and that there was a need for international standards for survival equipment. Because SOLAS standards are international, they tend to be high. Nations can set higher or lower standards than SOLAS for use within their own countries, but for international use safety equipment must meet SOLAS standards. SOLAS-approved equipment will often meet the requirement of another country you are traveling to.

SURVIVAL KITS

If you fall overboard or abandon ship quickly, do you have anything in your pockets or on you that would help you? A **personal survival kit** in a small waterproof container can speed up your rescue and make your life more tolerable in the meantime.

Think **small** (it's going in your pocket) and personalize your kit for your needs, and for the waters and shores where you are likely to be. Minimally, your kit should contain something from the following four categories:

◆ **Shelter:** Carry things that will help you make a shelter from your environment like large garbage bags, emergency foil blanket, twine, dental floss, nylon cord, etc.

◆ **Signals:** You want to get rescued! What about a strobe light, mini-B EPIRB, small flares, a mirror, whistle, light sticks, or surveyor's tape?

Survival kit.

◆ **Personal health needs:** This is where your kit really gets personal with items like medications you must take, aspirin, tampons, spare contact lenses, etc. You might want to add some food.

◆ **Fire:** If you are likely to end up on shore in a remote area, it helps to add a **fire starting device** that will work even if it's wet. Choices can include a lighter, fire starting sticks or bricks, candles, etc.

Carry a knife or utility tool!

ABANDON SHIP KITS

Larger than a personal survival kit, your abandon ship kit can contain more and larger items that make rescue more efficient and survival more tolerable. The container should be waterproof, floatable, have a convenient handle, and be stored where it can be easily grabbed in an emergency. A plastic five gallon bucket that can be tightly sealed, or a waterproof dry bag are two good choices.

Select items from the same four categories listed above for the personal survival kit. You might want to expand your signals to include a waterproof VHF radio, EPIRB, and larger flares. Water and food also could be added. An abandon ship kit can make your emergency much more survivable, but remember that you may not get to it and it does not take the place of your personal survival kit in your pocket.

By the way, do you and others on board know how to use all this stuff? You can learn a lot by reading the directions! Training will help, too. **Studies show that training is more important than any other factor in determining whether a person will react positively in an emergency.** There are many hands-on and online courses to choose from.

Dressing for Success!

Clothing is your first line of defense against the elements, and should be suitable for the environment you are going out in. A good rule for dressing on board is to consider the temperature of the water. One slip or fall and you could find yourself in a much colder environment than you planned!

Consider the **color** of your clothing. Does it make you more visible at night or if you fall in the water?

Fabrics? In warm climates cotton is great, **as long as it doesn't get wet.** Because cotton readily absorbs water and other liquids, as soon as it gets wet it loses most of its ability to trap air and keep you warm. **Cotton will not help keep you warm in the water.**

Polypropylene, other low absorption fabrics, polyester, or wool are essential for cool and cold boating climates because they help keep you warm, even when they are wet. Polypropylene is twice as warm as wool per pound, it dries out much quicker and it does not soak up as much water as wool. But synthetic fabrics do have a drawback—they melt!

Dressing in layers can also be helpful. Air gets trapped between the layers, increasing your insulation. Plus, layers allow you to shed or add clothing depending on the needs of the day.

The old expression, "If you feel cold, put on a hat." is true, so have a warm hat or hood. If you don't need it during the day, you probably will at night.

Some jacket or vest-style PFDs can serve as clothing. Pockets to hold deck and emergency gear are a plus and should be considered.

D. Brenner

ORIENTATION

Once you have thought about your boat, the people on board, where you are going, the environment, your equipment, and what can go wrong, it's time to share that information with others. **You should not be the only one on board who is familiar with your boat and equipment.** That might be good for your ego, but it will not help in an emergency, especially if something happens to you.

In 1991 the cruise liner *Oceanos* was in grave danger off the coast of South Africa when the captian abandoned the vessel before many of the 571 passengers! It was one of the ship's entertainers who manned the radio room and helped coordinate the rescue. In an emergency, **you** could end up playing a critical role.

The information you need to share in this orientation will depend on your boat and how complicated things are. A check list will help both you and passengers who look at it later.

The basic points in your orientation should include

◆ How to start, stop, and steer your boat, and how to shut off the fuel supply.

◆ Where the anchor is and how to set it in an emergency.

Here's a good reminder to see whether or not you are prepared for a safe trip:

When you call the Coast Guard ... you are asking them to risk their lives to save yours. The rescuers ... value their lives as much as we value ours. It is the duty of those who go to sea to avoid getting into situations that require the aid of the rescue services—heed the season, equip your vessel properly, keep a sharp eye for weather changes, shake down a new vessel conscientiously, don't expect your ship to do something she can't, pump for your life if you're sinking, maneuver your vessel if you're not. Think ahead. Anything less and you will be asking more of others than you ask of yourself.

"The Abandonment of the John F. Leavitt"
by Peter Spectre, Woodenboat Magazine

◆ How to use the stove, including how to shut it off.

◆ Where the fire extinguishers are.

◆ Putting on PFDs, and where the immersion suits (if on board) are.

◆ How to broadcast a Mayday. (Put a Mayday information sticker on or near your radio.)

◆ How to launch your survival craft.

◆ How to use and detach your EPIRB (if you have one) from its bracket so you can take it with you in an abandon ship emergency.

◆ How to get someone back on board.

◆ Where the first aid and abandon ship kits are.

◆ Where you are going, and how much fun it is going to be!

Do everything you can to prepare for a safe trip.

Sea Grant
Alaska

BUSINESS REPLY MAIL

First Class Mail   Permit No. 13   Fairbanks, AK

POSTAGE WILL BE PAID BY ADDRESSEE

Alaska Sea Grant College Program
P.O. Box 755040
University of Alaska Fairbanks
Fairbanks, AK 99775-9988

Dear Reader of

Please let the publisher know what you think of this book. If you have recommendations for changes that would make the book more useful, please tell us!

Yes No Is the information in the book well organized?
Yes No Is the book interesting to read?
Yes No Does the book cover a well balanced range of boating safety topics?
Yes No Did the information in the book help you learn safe boating practices?
Yes No Did you find any inaccuracies in the book? (If you did, list them below.)
Yes No Where did you get this book? _____
What would you add, delete, or change to improve the book?

_____

What is the most important thing you learned from the book?

_____

Comments: *(Please write us a letter or send e-mail to FNSK@uaf.edu if you have more to say! Use zip code 99775-5040 on letters.)*

Name _____
Title / Organization _____
Address _____
City _____ State _____ Zip_____
Country _____

Reading the Weather

D. Brenner

When that nice clear morning turns into a rainy, windy afternoon—spoiling your day—are you taken by surprise? Knowing how to get the most out of National Weather Service broadcasts, how to read weather maps, and make and interpret your own weather observations can help you make wiser boating decisions. Understanding some weather basics and terminology is the first step.

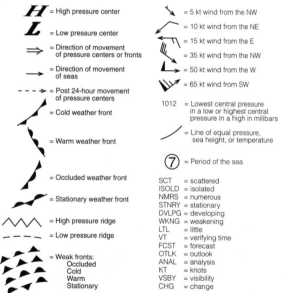

National Weather Service symbols and abbreviations.

WEATHER BROADCASTS AND MAPS
High and Low Pressure

The air in the earth's atmosphere constantly moves to equalize temperature differences between the earth's air, water, and land masses. As these bodies of warm and cold air circulate they build up areas of low and high pressure, which are represented on weather maps by the letters L and H. Low pressure systems usually bring poor or worsening weather, while high pressure systems generally produce good or improving weather.

In the Northern Hemisphere, detailed maps also show that air flows clockwise around high pressure systems, and counterclockwise around low pressure systems. This air flow is caused by the earth's rotation and is reversed in the Southern Hemisphere.

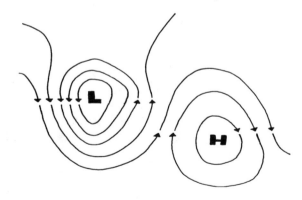

Air flow in the Northern Hemisphere.

On weather maps, high and low pressure systems have lines—isobars—drawn around them to connect places of equal barometric pressure. Isobars not only show the shape of a weather system, but also give some indication of surface wind strength. Closer isobars mean stronger winds because there is a greater difference in air pressure in a shorter distance.

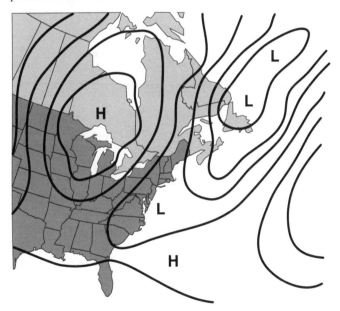

High and low pressure over eastern North America, and Atlantic Ocean.

Fronts

Cold and warm air masses do not tend to mix, so they usually have a boundary—called a front—between them. Fronts are important to track because that is where storms develop.

Meteorologists use symbols to distinguish the four kinds of fronts: cold, warm, stationary, and occluded. Cold air moving toward warm air is called a **cold front**, and is represented by a line with triangles on its leading edge. **Warm fronts**, depicted by a line with semicircles on its leading edge, occur when warm air moves toward cold air. When a cold front overtakes a warm front, the result is an **occluded front**, and is shown by a line with both triangles and semicircles on its leading edge. If a front becomes **stationary**, the semicircles and triangles are drawn on opposite sides of the line.

Although land formations can alter a weather system's course, the systems generally travel from west to east in the Northern Hemisphere. This, too, is caused by the earth's rotation.

Cold weather front Warm weather front Occluded weather front Stationary weather front

Wind Warnings

The National Weather Service (NWS) issues four categories of wind warnings: small craft advisories, gale warnings, storm warnings, and hurricane winds.

♦ A **small craft advisory** is a prediction for winds from 18 to 33 knots (21-38 mph).

♦ **Gale warnings** forecast winds from 34 to 47 knots (39-54 mph).

♦ **Storm warnings** predict winds of 48 to 63 knots (55-73 mph).

♦ **Hurricane winds** are 64 knots (74 mph) and above.

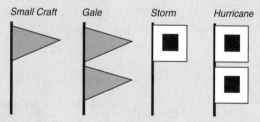

Small Craft   Gale   Storm   Hurricane

(Note: The NWS uses the hurricane winds category only in those parts of the United States that normally have hurricanes. For non-hurricane areas, storm warnings are for winds of 48 knots and above.)

The wind forecast also includes a prediction on wind direction.

Sea Height Forecasts

The NWS also issues sea height forecasts for coastal areas—for average sea height conditions to be encountered in open coastal waters unless otherwise indicated. The forecasted sea height is the average height of the highest one-third of the expected waves—although waves can occasionally combine and reach heights of twice the forecast value. Sea height values do not take into account areas of normally higher or steeper seas found near bars, shoals, or restricted entrances into sounds or inlets. If you are not familiar with these variations where you will be boating, ask other mariners. Local knowledge may save you some very unpleasant boating experiences!

Listening to Forecasts

If you carefully listen to weather broadcasts two or three times daily, and use an actual or mental map of your area to picture where the weather fronts and systems are located and how they are moving in relation to your position or destination, you will have a clear idea of the changes in store for your area. Write down the pertinent information; memories can be weak.

Marine weather broadcasts often include a synopsis of weather systems and a 12 to 24 hour outlook. Sometimes a three to five day outlook is included. NWS broadcasts and weather radiofacsimiles are available for all coastal areas. Locate the most convenient source (a VHF or SSB radio weather broadcast, local AM or FM radio broadcasts, or reports in harbors) and make listening to these forecasts a part of your boating routine. (The National Weather Service has a web site where you can access forecasts and a host of other interesting information: **www.nws.noaa.gov.**) If you are operating in foreign waters, learn sources of reliable weather reports and ask other boaters what the local weather indicators are for waters you will be visiting. You can learn a lot from the experience and mistakes of other boaters.

You should never rely on just a single source of information for a weather forecast. Radio reports, cloud formations, weather charts, local knowledge, and what you are feeling in your face are all important parts of the equation that make up weather forecasting.

When you are deciding whether or not to leave, try not to let a desire to get to your destination overrule good judgment. Many lives have been lost by boaters who "just had to get there" at a certain time or day. The weather isn't going to consult you! Try to plan some flexible time in your cruise so you are not tempted to try to outrun a weather front.

USING LOCAL OBSERVATIONS TO SUPPLEMENT FORECASTS

Reading the Barometer

Although a barometer does nothing more than measure air pressure, it can be a valuable tool, especially if you read it regularly, record the readings, and remember that air pressure is only one part of the total weather picture.

Lightning

In many areas, the boating season corresponds with the thunderstorm season, with the storms and their accompanying lightning often coming on suddenly. Being on the water makes you an excellent target for a lightning strike, which can damage electronic equipment and your vessel, or seriously injure or kill people on board. The type of lightning protection you need depends on your vessel. For smaller vessels, the most prudent step may be to get passengers ashore to safety. If you are not sure how to protect yourself and your vessel from lightning, consider contacting the American Boat and Yacht Council, or American Fire Protection Association. American Boat and Yacht Council, 3069 Solomon's Island Rd., Edgewater, MD, 21037, (410) 956-1050.

To Get the Most out of Your Barometer

◆ Read it at least twice a day. Gently tap the barometer's face, and watch which way the needle moves. The tapping releases the stored up friction and usually makes the pointer jump slightly up or down, although the needle will move by itself with larger changes of air pressure.

◆ Record the reading, the time, and how much the pressure has changed since the last reading. This can go in your ship's log as a permanent record.

◆ After you have taken your reading, set the moveable needle on top of the pressure needle so you have a reference point for your next reading. This will tell you whether air pressure is rising or falling, and how rapidly it is changing.

General Barometric Pressure Rules

◆ Falling barometric pressure means poor or worsening weather. The faster the fall, the stronger the storm.

◆ Rising pressure usually indicates clearing or good weather. The faster the rise, the sooner the clearing (which can be accompanied by high winds).

◆ When the barometer has been reading exceptionally high for a few days, weather changes occur slowly.

◆ Tides are somewhat affected by air pressure. The air in a high pressure system is **heavier** than in a low pressure, so it pushes down on the ocean more than a low does. Consequently, when the weather is dominated by a very high pressure system, the water level won't fluctuate as much, and high tides are often **lower** than predicted.

During a strong low pressure system the air does not exert as much weight on the ocean, so the high tides can rise more. This, combined with the driving winds associated with intense low pressure systems, often creates damaging storm tides.

Clouds

Observation of cloud types and movement is an important component of making your own weather predictions. Although this chapter does not detail the various types of clouds, following are some general observations:

◆ Thickening and lowering clouds signal the approach of wet weather.

◆ High, thin clouds can be an early sign of approaching bad weather.

◆ Fair weather will generally continue when cloud bases increase in height along mountains.

General Weather Observations

- The weather will generally worsen when the wind shifts to the south or east.

- Fair weather will usually continue when there is heavy dew or frost at night, the moon shines brightly, and the wind is light. The latter conditions are also often associated with a falling temperature.

- The temperature will usually fall when the wind shifts into or continues to blow northerly or northwesterly, or when the barometer rises steadily in the winter. Conversely, the temperature will rise when the wind shifts from the west or northwest to the south.

- To locate the center of the storm, use Buys Ballot's law of wind and pressure. In the Northern Hemisphere, face the true wind (not the apparent wind caused by the combination of the true wind and the wind caused by the vessel's own forward motion) and stretch out your arms. According to Buys Ballot's law, the center of the low pressure will be to your right and somewhat behind you.

The center of the high pressure will be to your left and somewhat in front of you. This method can help you track the path of a weather system. Many mariners commit this to memory: "Wind in your face, low to your right."

- In coastal waters, weather is modified by many local factors including mountain ranges, islands, glaciers, and coastal currents. Learn your local weather indicators.

- Make weather observations often, noting both the current weather and any changes that have occurred.

Locate the center of the storm by using Buys Ballot's law. This law was formulated in 1857 by the Dutch meteorologist Buys Ballot, and is also know as the Baric Wind law.

Fog

◆ **Radiation fog** occurs in near-calm, clear weather when the earth loses heat into the night air, cooling and condensing the air above it. Depending on the wind, radiation fog can be anywhere from two to several hundred feet thick. It begins to evaporate shortly after sunrise, with the lower layers going first, but is slow to clear over water.

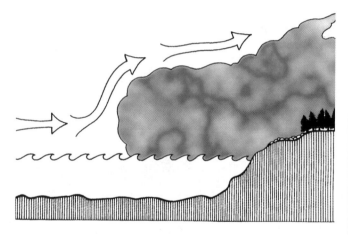

Development of advection fog.

◆ When warm, moist air blows over cooler surfaces such as land or coastal water, the result is **advection fog**. This type of fog may develop day or night, winter or summer, over the ocean and is the most likely type to be encountered at sea. Unfortunately, advection fog does not dissipate readily, and usually doesn't clear unless the wind shifts or increases dramatically in speed. Sunshine has no effect on advection fog over water.

◆ **Steam fog**, also known as arctic sea smoke, develops when very cold arctic air (less than 10°F) blows over warmer water.

◆ If fog persists after 1 or 2 pm and no major weather changes have taken place, the fog will remain and probably become thicker.

Talk to locals and mariners with experience on the waters where you intend to travel; they have a wealth of information about local weather patterns.

Combine your observations with official forecasts to avoid as much heavy weather as possible. Seasoned boaters know that heavy weather can turn a relatively uneventful trip into a life and death situation.

Courtesy of Clark County Sheriff's Office, Marine Patrol Program, Vancouver, WA.

Arkansas River, Colorado: Three men in a six-foot inflatable boat were headed down the Arkansas River when they hit a class II rapid and were thrown into the water. Two of the men were wearing PFDs, the third was not, despite the fact that there was one for him in the boat. The man without the PFD drowned.

Earlier that day a Colorado State Park Ranger had seen the boaters and recommended that they all don PFDs. The man without one asked, "Is it a requirement that I wear it?" and he was told, "No." He then refused to put it on even though he could not swim. After his death he was found to have a blood alcohol content of 0.125%, which is above the legal limit to be considered intoxicated.

Alcohol is just one thing that can endanger a mariner, both by affecting his judgment and possibly contributing to the loss of his boat or life. Seasickness and fatigue can also put you at risk. Read on for some suggestions on what to do about these three problems at sea.

ALCOHOL, DRUGS, AND BOATING

The fact that over 50% of boating casualties are alcohol related shows that alcohol and substance abuse are problems in the recreational boating world, just like in other walks of life.

The effects of drinking alcohol while boating have been clearly demonstrated by skippers who volunteered for an experiment that measured their ability to operate a boat under the influence. Despite the fact that all of the volunteers felt that their performance improved, both observers and objective measurements indicated that it actually decreased. Not only did the skippers perform poorly, but their judgment of their own condition was faulty after they consumed alcohol.

Alcohol is not the only drug that causes problems among boaters. Amphetamines, cocaine, and other drugs are all too common. Some can produce a rush that allows you to stay awake for hours on end, but they are highly addictive and can impair judgment. Prescription and over-the-counter drugs can also cause problems. Know what you're taking and follow medication precautions.

There are many reasons why alcohol and boating just don't mix:

◆ Alcohol lowers inhibitions and increases risk taking. This effect is one of the things that makes drinking appealing to some people, but when **loss of judgment** is combined with unforgiving waters it equals fatalities.

- There's a reason that people who have been drinking are called "tipsy." Alcohol causes you to **lose your sense of balance.** Most of us have seen drunk, staggering people. Imagine them in rough seas, or trying to make their way down the dock, or from boat to boat in the harbor. Having people on board who have a decreased sense of balance due to alcohol consumption isn't just dangerous for the drinker; it's a liability for the vessel's owner/operator and other passengers.

- Alcohol causes your blood vessels to dilate (expand), which encourages heat loss. That's why many people look and feel flushed when they drink. The warm glow you feel when drinking is actually the glow of heat leaving your body. As a rule, when in the water a person who has been drinking will succumb to **hypothermia** sooner than one who has not.

- Alcohol acts as a central nervous system depressant and **slows reaction time.**

- **Alcohol affects your vision.** It reduces night vision, peripheral vision, and the ability to see clearly. It also lessens the ability to distinguish between red and black.

- Alcohol **increases the chances of becoming disoriented and drowning when suddenly immersed in cold water.**

- Drunken, belligerent people can **ruin a voyage** in more ways than one.

Boating Under the Influence

Operating a vessel while intoxicated became a federal offense in 1988. If blood alcohol content is 0.10% (0.08% in some states) or higher, violators are subject to a fine and imprisonment.

In many states, a conviction for drinking while driving a boat will count against your automobile driving record. If you already have a DWI conviction in an automobile and get another one while operating a vessel, it will count as your second conviction. A designated driver can be a good start, but it is extremely dangerous to have incapacitated people on board who will not be able to help themselves or others in the event of an emergency.

All of these are good reasons to have an alcohol policy for your vessel. Here are some sample policies used by skippers:

◆ No alcohol allowed on board.

◆ Alcohol consumption limited to 1-2 drinks per person per day.

◆ Alcohol consumed only when anchored or tied up for the day.

◆ 12 hours from bottle to throttle. (Many airplane pilots adhere to this one.)

◆ No alcohol for the captain or crew.

Alcohol and boating just don't mix.

FATIGUE

What does fatigue have to do with boating? A lot! Fatigue negatively affects mood, the ability to concentrate, and complex thinking ability, including decision making. The ability to do useful mental work declines 25% for every 14 hours a person is awake. In short, tired people are careless, less attentive, less capable of making quick decisions, and a liability to themselves and fellow passengers.

Adding to these problems is something called boater's hypnosis: a fatigue that can be brought on by just four hours' exposure to the noise, vibration, sun, glare, wind, and motion that occurs while on the water. Boater's hypnosis slows reaction time as much as being legally drunk. It also (at least) doubles the effects of alcohol, so one drink on board is equal to two or more on shore.

According to the U.S. Coast Guard, 80% of boating casualties are caused by human error, and one of the main contributors to human error is fatigue.

Extensive research has been conducted on the effects of sleep deprivation on human performance and what we can do about it. Here is what we know:

Effects of Sleep Loss

Each of us has an internal biological clock that establishes our daily rhythm of physical and psychological actions. Our bodies tend to want to follow this routine even when our normal sleep-wake cycle is altered. As part of our daily rhythm, our alertness and stamina normally reach their daily low between 2 am and 6 am, when we are usually asleep. When we don't sleep during these hours our work performance declines, the effects of sleep loss are amplified, and it's much more likely that accidents will occur.

Although it is difficult to predict how sleep loss will affect an individual, the majority of researchers agree that the most significant effects of sleep loss are psychological. Since most people need six to eight hours of sleep each night, missing just one regular sleep cycle can cause us to become more irritable, depressed, disoriented, and unable to concentrate.

Sleep experts have found several direct links between sleep loss and performance.

◆ **Interesting jobs are less likely to be affected by sleep loss than boring jobs.** Boating in extremely heavy seas or when the fishing is hot might be interesting enough to ward off many of the negative effects of lack of sleep, but boating on calm seas with little sleep can make for such boring conditions that performance can decline.

◆ **New and complex skills are often more seriously affected by lack of sleep than simple tasks that are second nature.**

◆ **Sleep loss slows reaction time.** This can be a dangerous situation when precision is needed to work with equipment in rough seas, or steer in rough or confused seas.

◆ **As sleep loss increases, performance becomes more uneven.** This means that a tired person who is performing well—and appears to be okay—may lapse into unsafe behaviors with no warning.

◆ **Most people take 10 to 15 minutes to fully function after waking up.** This can be a dangerous time.

How can you maximize your effectiveness when you spend long hours on the water?

◆ Anything that increases psychological arousal, or enhances mood and motivation, improves job performance. This is especially true during the 2 am to 6 am low.

◆ Rotate jobs to help keep sleepy minds awake.

◆ Wake people at least 15 minutes before they need to stand watch or perform other activities that require them to think.

◆ Overlap watches to make sure the new person is awake and alerted to any upcoming hazards.

◆ Increase arousal by exercising to increase circulation and oxygen intake, breathing fresh air, listening to high-spirited music, splashing cold water on your face, chewing flavored bubble gum, standing rather than sitting during wheel watches, and drinking soda pop or non-alcoholic drinks.

◆ Brushing your teeth, washing up, or quickly shampooing your hair can improve your mood and help keep you awake as can stimulating your sense of smell with aftershave, soaps, and hand lotion. Humor can also be extremely effective in improving mood.

◆ Bodies, like boats, need a source of energy to run. Eating well and drinking enough water is critical when you are low on sleep because your performance will drop even more if you are dehydrated. If you're a quart low on your fluid intake, you've lost up to one-third of your physical strength and mental sharpness. If you want to feel better and have a sustained level of energy, drink enough healthy liquids (2-4 quarts a day!), and eat three meals a day that include protein, carbohydrates, and some fat.

Get Some Rest!

One of the major conclusions from sleep loss research is that the only sure way to completely recover from sleep deprivation is—you guessed it—to sleep. Five to twelve hours of uninterrupted sleep allows most people to recover from even many days without sleep. So try to sleep when you can.

Taking steps to decrease sleep loss problems can make the difference between getting to harbor tired or arriving seriously injured or dead.

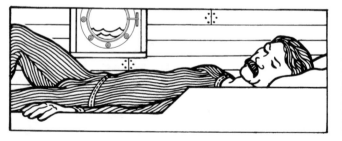

SEASICKNESS

Sooner or later "enfermo del mar" strikes every mariner. Back at the dock, we often make light of these attacks, but extended seasickness can cause massive dehydration, loss of your will to live, and death.

If you are prone to seasickness there are some preventive measures you can take:

◆ Start your voyage with a positive attitude. Positive thinking alone may not prevent a visit to the rail, but convincing yourself ahead of time that you **will** be afflicted does not help.

◆ Stay on deck in a well-ventilated area, and keep your eyes on the horizon, if possible. Some people find that they feel fine as long as they do not read or do detail work.

◆ Place yourself in a stable part of the vessel like the cockpit rather than the flying bridge.

◆ For some people, lying down helps. For others it only makes matters worse.

◆ Avoid greasy, spicy foods, alcohol, tobacco, dairy products, caffeine, and fuel smells, if possible.

◆ In almost all cases, people do better if they have a little bland food like plain crackers in their stomachs.

◆ Some people find relief in acupressure bracelets or ginger.

◆ If you think you may be seasick on a trip, plan ahead. Most seasickness medications must be taken one hour in advance to be effective. Many people find the two-drug combination of ephedrine and promethazine to be the most effective with the least amount of side effects, but check with your physician to determine what will help you the most.

◆ In the early stages of seasickness you may be able to reverse its course by getting fresh air, eating bland crackers, drinking flat clear soda like ginger-ale, or getting off the boat!

◆ If seasickness progresses to the vomiting stage, it will take one of two paths. The first is that after vomiting for a while, you get your sea legs and recover. Many long-time boaters have bouts of seasickness at the beginning of a voyage and then are "cured" for the boating season.

◆ The second and more dangerous path is that you continue to vomit. After 12 hours of this, dehydration can become serious and you should return to shore. If this is not possible, seasickness medications in suppository form may be in order just to keep liquids down. In extreme cases you may need to contact a physician.

You can do a lot to minimize your risks on board.

D. Brenner

A 25-year-old Icelandic man survived by swimming 5 hours in 40°F water after his vessel was lost in below-freezing temperatures. Researchers say that the man's body type, youth, excellent physical condition, and body fat were critical in his survival.

E very year thousands of people end up unexpectedly in the water. Some disappear in just a few minutes while others survive for hours or even days until they are rescued. What makes the difference? A number of factors influence your in-water survival time: the temperature of the water, your body type, your general physical condition, types of injuries, the kind of clothes you are wearing, what activity you are doing while in the water, and your will to survive.

Immersion suits help retain body heat in water.

AMSEA

To understand these factors better, it helps to know where your body's high heat loss areas are, and how your body gains and loses heat.

HIGH HEAT LOSS AREAS

Your body has five major heat loss areas:

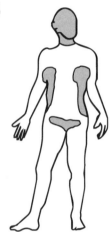

- Head (responsible for 50% of heat loss)

- Neck

- Armpits

- Sides of chest

- Groin

Although your hands and feet may be the first to feel cold, they are not major heat loss sources.

HOW YOUR BODY GAINS AND LOSES HEAT

Your body operates at its prime within a very narrow temperature range of only two or so degrees. It has only three ways to gain heat but five different ways to lose it.

Heat Gain

Your body gains heat three ways:

◆ **External sources:** The sun, fires, and other heat sources warm your body.

◆ **Digestion:** Heat is produced as your body digests food.

◆ **Muscular activity:** As you move, your body produces heat, **but** activity in cold water may cause you to lose more heat than you gain because cold water is constantly flowing past your body's high heat loss areas.

Heat Loss

Your body can lose heat five different ways:

◆ **Radiation:** Radiation occurs when heat is emitted from your body. Clothing is the obvious answer to preventing heat loss through radiation. Some fabrics are better than others at doing this.

◆ **Respiration:** Respiration is the answer to, "Why do dogs pant so hard on a hot day?" You lose heat by exhaling air that your body has warmed. Some of this heat loss can be prevented by covering your mouth with a loose knit scarf, hat, or other fabric.

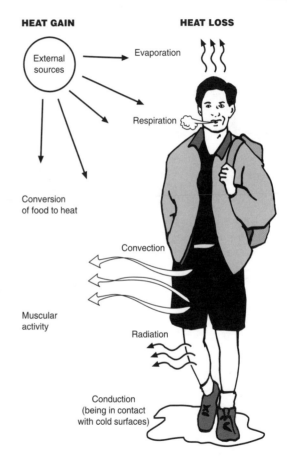

HEAT GAIN   HEAT LOSS

External sources

Evaporation

Respiration

Conversion of food to heat

Convection

Muscular activity

Radiation

Conduction (being in contact with cold surfaces)

◆ **Evaporation:** When your sweat evaporates, your body loses heat and moisture into the air. This explains why wet clothes make you cooler, which can be good in a hot climate but deadly in a cool one.

◆ **Conduction:** Being in direct contact with cold surfaces—either solids or liquids—takes your body heat away. Insulating yourself from these cold surfaces will stop or greatly slow conductive heat loss.

◆ **Convection:** Why does it feel cooler on windy days? Convection! This happens when your body's heat is taken away by **moving** air or water.

The combination of conduction and convection is the reason **your body loses heat 25 times faster in water than in air of the same temperature.**

Not being able to control your body's heat loss can lead to hypothermia, the lowering of your body's core temperature, which is one of the leading killers outdoors. For information on how to treat it, see page 138.

FACTORS THAT AFFECT IN-WATER SURVIVAL

Water Temperature

One of the most important factors in water survival is temperature. All things being equal, your chances of surviving are much better in warm water than cold water. But just how cold is cold water?

For the body to maintain a temperature of 98.6°F, and survive an extended period of immersion, the water must be above 91°F. The relatively thin layer of fat in the average human is not sufficient to protect the body from heat loss due to contact with colder and moving water. So by this definition, **cold water is any water below 91°F.**

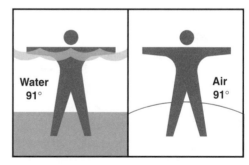

Your body loses heat 25 times faster in the water than in air of the same temperature.

However, muscle movement, such as swimming, generates heat. Thus, through exercise we can maintain our body temperature in water temperatures down to 72°F . The catch, however, is that rest and food are needed for heat production.

Immersion in water below 70°F can profoundly affect the body's metabolism and lead to drowning. For more information on drowning, see page 129.

Body Type

Certain rare individuals, such as the 5-foot 6-inch, 209-pound cold water distance swimmer Lynne Cox, are able to maintain their body temperature in even colder water due to their body type (an estimated 40% of her body is fat). Yet her aerobic capacity is estimated to be that of a world-class marathon runner. People with insulating layers of fat who are also superb athletes are the usual long distance swimmer types.

But just because you're skinny, it does not mean you are going to die if you find yourself in water for extended periods of time. A positive mental attitude can make all the difference!

General Physical Condition/Injuries

Generally, people who are in good physical condition and have fewer injuries are more likely to survive extended times in the water. But never underestimate an injured person's will to live, even if they are not in top condition.

Type of Clothes

Think wool, polypropylene, or other fabrics that keep you warm even when wet. **Cotton will not.** (See Chapter 1, Preparing for a Safe Trip, for more information on clothing.) Immersion suits or deck coveralls (see Chapter 5, PFDs) can also greatly extend your in-water survival time.

In-Water Activity

Should you try to swim to shore? The decision to swim, or to remain still to conserve energy and reduce heat loss, is a judgment call in all situations and depends on the factors mentioned above. When swimming is appropriate, try your most proficient swim stroke. Unless the crawl stroke is easy and natural for you, you will probably find that a back or breast stroke will be less tiring. In either case, you need to take into account the nearness of rescue as well as the temperature of the water, the tides, currents, distance to shore, and your swimming ability before you decide to swim your way out of a problem situation.

Will to Survive

You've read it repeatedly: your will to survive can make the difference between life and death. It is well documented that depression lowers your body core temperature and reduces your will to live. So think positive thoughts about people, pets, or possessions that you want to see again. Decide to go for the *Guinness Book of World Records*!

HOW TO EXTEND YOUR IN-WATER SURVIVAL TIME

You can extend your in-water survival time by getting yourself out of the water as soon as possible and reducing your body's heat loss by following the **Stay Rules.**

◆ **Signal** for help as soon as possible. This is where the whistle, flare, or other signals you put on your PFD will come in handy. (You did do that, didn't you?) Yell and wave your arms. Put the hood up on your float coat, coveralls, or foul weather gear; they are often bright and some have reflective tape on them. Make yourself as visible as possible. The people on the boat need to know you are overboard before they can help you.

◆ **Stay with the boat.** Make sure you do not abandon your vessel until being on board is more dangerous than being in the water. If your boat does capsize, beware of entrapment, anything that could snag you, and hazardous floating debris.

Once capsized, many vessels float due to air trapped inside their hulls. Plus, all commercially made monohull recreational vessels under 20 feet (except canoes, kayaks, inflatables, and sailboats) built after July 31, 1978 are constructed so that some portion of the vessel will float above water when it is swamped or capsized. The amount of flotation put into the boat is determined by whether it is built for an outboard or inboard/outboard engine, the engine size, and the passenger and weight carrying capacity. **Do not** remove this flotation!

Staying with your vessel also makes you a bigger target for rescuers, and keeps you closer to your last reported position.

◆ **Stay afloat.** Staying afloat is critical, but how do you stay afloat when your vessel has been lost? With your PFD!

Your body has only a few air spaces—your lungs and stomach—to aid in buoyancy, so anything that floats you higher will help you avoid swallowing or inhaling water. Wearing a PFD also greatly reduces your risk of panic and helps you control the involuntary gasping that can occur in cold water.

Whether or not to remove clothing and boots when you are in the water is controversial. Leaving clothes on traps air and keeps you warmer, but movement will allow the air to escape. Boots and waders can be buoyant if they are sealed well by clothing and bent knees.

In colder waters it might be advantageous to leave on clothes and boots as long as possible and remain still to minimize loss of air between layers. In warmer waters, clothes may be removed and filled with air to serve as a flotation aid, but this should **only** be used as a warm water technique.

Sinking boats leave much debris in their wake that can also help you stay afloat and get higher out of the water: ice chests, fenders, buoys, jerry jugs, and other buoyant items. In one case, people from a sunken vessel in the Pacific tied all of the vessel's buoys together and made a raft that floated them for days!

◆ **Stay dry.** Water robs heat from your body 25 times faster than air of the same temperature, so do anything you can to stay dry. Immersion suits are the only type of flotation device that is designed to keep you dry, and they should be seriously considered by all boaters on cold waters.

If you have to enter the water, do it slowly. This will keep you drier and help you control your breathing. Sudden immersion in cold water can sometimes lead to what is called the Sudden Drowning Syndrome, where cold water gets into your ear, causing you to lose your sense of direction. This partially explains why even strong swimmers sometimes drown in cold water.

Since 50% of your body's heat loss is from your head, keep your head as dry as possible. Especially **avoid** using the "drown proofing" technique of holding your breath and submerging your head under water when you are in cold water. This is one of the quickest ways to cool off. Instead, get as much of your body as possible out of the water.

◆ **Stay still.** Body movement increases heat production, but this can either help or hurt you depending on the temperature of the water. In cooler water, less exercise is better. If you stay still you lose less heat—by as much as 30%—than if you are swimming or treading water.

◆ **Stay warm.** Think about what you wear boating. Will it keep you warm if you end up in the water? Wool, polypropylene, and similar fabrics will. Cotton will not.

Prolong your survival time by protecting your high heat loss areas: head, neck, armpits, sides of the chest and groin. If you have a PFD, assume the Heat Escape Lessening Position (HELP) if you are alone or the HUDDLE position if you are in a group. (Put very young, injured, and elderly people in the middle if you can.) These positions will **double** your in-water survival time.

HELP position.

In rough waters, you will need to drop your legs straight down to maintain stability in the HELP position. Keep your thighs together, ankles crossed, and arms next to your sides. Cross your arms on your chest; grasping your knees will tend to put your face in the water.

If you have a PFD with an inflatable bladder, inflate it as soon as you are in the water!

Some survivors have complained of being too hot in their immersion suits. The excitement and activity of abandoning ship can make you feel hot, especially if you have several layers of clothes on under your suit. Even if you are tempted to open the suit to cool off, **don't!** It is important to stay as dry as possible. Getting soaked from sweat is not good, but it is better than having a lot of water in your suit.

◆ **Stay together.** Staying together has several benefits. It allows you to share body heat if you are in a Huddle, to boost each other's morale, to check on each other's condition, and it makes you a bigger target for rescuers. The will to survive can be much stronger when your friends and loved ones are at hand, as opposed to wondering where they have drifted off to and if they are still okay. Help each other. It's harder to give up when you are part of a team.

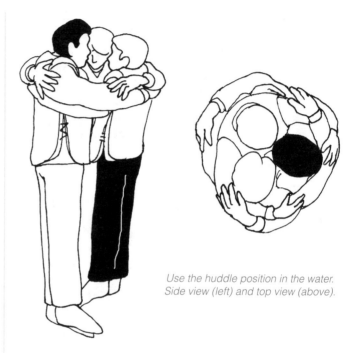

Use the huddle position in the water. Side view (left) and top view (above).

If you need to swim, do it as a team by tandem swimming on your back.

Stay together by tandem swimming.

◆ **Stay sober.** Alcohol is linked to at least 50% of all recreational boating fatalities. It is a bad idea to drink and boat. See Chapter 3, Alcohol, Fatigue and Seasickness, for more information.

Remember, if you are in the water when you don't want to be, your job is to **signal for help, stay afloat, and conserve heat.**

How to Be a Survivor

For all of the pleasure boating gives us, it occurs in an environment hostile to human life. At one time it was widely believed that if you fell in the water you were dead, but we now know that this is not necessarily true. Being prepared with a PFD, and knowing what actions to take in the water will help you be a survivor!

Courtesy of AMSEA

Bayou Teche, Louisiana—A 32-year-old man and a 5-year-old boy were traveling in a 12-foot aluminum boat with a 15 hp engine when they struck a log. The boat capsized and the two were thrown into the water. The boy, who was wearing a Type II PFD, survived by holding onto the boat. The man drowned trying to swim to the bank. He was not wearing a PFD, despite the fact that there was one in the boat.

It happens more than we like to admit. Boaters end up in the water when they don't want to—some because they had to abandon ship, others because they were drunk, and a surprising number because they were standing at the rail relieving themselves.

Whatever the cause, the result is the same—the water is cold. Any water below 91°F will make you hypothermic unless you get out of the water or are protected from the cold. Water robs heat from your body 25 times faster than air of the same temperature. Even expert swimmers can drown or die from hypothermia if they are not wearing a personal flotation device (PFD).

Unless you can guarantee that you will not end up in the water, you must know how to prolong your in-water survival time. This is where PFDs play their part.

A study of fully investigated recreational boating fatalities showed that **more than 85% of the people who died were not wearing a personal flotation device.** The fact is **your chances of surviving are much higher if you are wearing a PFD.**

CHOOSING A PFD

Boaters now have a wide variety of styles and colors to choose from, **so select a PFD that you will wear.** PFDs are like parachutes—they work best when you have them on!

Consider the following when you evaluate your options: buoyancy, hypothermia protection, fit, comfort, visibility, cost, features, your boating activity, type of vessel plus legal requirements for your vessel and onboard children.

D. Brenner

Today's PFDs are comfortable and stylish, and they work!

Buoyancy

Keep in mind that the more pounds of buoyancy a PFD has, the higher out of the water you will float, thereby increasing your chances of survival—especially in rough seas. Pounds of buoyancy has no relationship to how much a PFD weighs. It refers to the Archimedes principle: an object is buoyed up by a force equal to the weight of the water it displaces.

Wearing your PFD in the water is the only way to determine if it will float you with your mouth well out of the water. Since you will probably try this out on a calm day, remember to factor in a good margin for rougher water!

Hypothermia Protection

Hypothermia protection is highest when the five high heat loss areas—the head, neck, armpits, sides of the chest, and groin—can be kept warm and dry. Some PFDs provide good hypothermia protection in calm waters, but are less effective in rough seas because body movement or the PFD design permit cold water to flush past the skin.

Fit

Make sure the PFD fits before you buy it. Try it on while wearing the clothes you normally wear on board, and adjust it so it's comfortable. If you are not sure how to adjust the one you are considering, ask a sales person. You are most likely to wear a PFD that fits and is comfortable.

Color

Bright colors are in fashion and being used by PFD manufacturers, so boaters have a wide variety of stylish PFDs which can increase their visibility in an emergency. Today, it is possible to find a PFD that will be comfortable in almost any situation on board, and make a fashion statement!

Cost, Features, and Boating Activity

PFDs vary in cost and features. You may choose a different PFD for an open boat than for a kayak or a cabin cruiser.

Legal Requirements

Many states require that children under a certain age wear a PFD while on deck or in an open cockpit of a recreational vessel. This is a good idea even if it isn't the law where you live.

The U.S. Coast Guard booklet *Federal Requirements and Safety Tips for Recreational Boats* includes PFD requirements. Find out what you need on your vessel by getting this publication from the Coast Guard, Coast Guard Auxiliary, or local marine supply store.

USCG-APPROVED PFDs

Type I PFD--Offshore Life Jacket

These are the PFDs that are commonly found on charter vessels, ferries, and cruise ships.

With a minimum of 22 pounds of buoyancy, adult Type I PFDs contain the most built-in flotation for their size. Since most of their flotation is positioned on the chest, they will turn most unconscious people (about 80%) face up in the water. However, Type I PFDs have only minimal hypothermia protection, and many people consider them too bulky. They do not provide as much hypothermia protection as float coats, coveralls, and immersion suits, but they are reversible—a nice feature if you need to put on one in a hurry.

The child size Type I has a minimum of 11 pounds of buoyancy.

Type I PFD—Offshore life jacket.

Type II PFD—Nearshore Buoyant Vest

Type II PFDs for adults have a minimum of 15.5 pounds of buoyancy, and will turn about 20% of unconscious people who wear them face up in the water. Type IIs offer little hypothermia protection and may be awkward to wear in some boating situations, but they are relatively inexpensive and provide a good alternative for parents who need to outfit growing children on a limited budget.

A medium child Type II provides at least 11 pounds of buoyancy, while small child and infant sizes must have a minimum of 7 pounds of buoyancy.

Type II PFD—Nearshore buoyant vest.

Type III PFD—Flotation Aid

There are several different styles of adult Type III PFDs, all of which have the same buoyancy as Type IIs, 15.5 pounds. The child and infant sizes provide the same buoyancy as their Type II counterparts. Unfortunately, they will not turn an unconscious person face up and they offer less hypothermia protection than float coats or flotation coveralls.

Some boaters use the Type III vest-style while kayaking, canoeing, waterskiing, or on deck because they allow fairly good mobility. If you are a waterskier make sure your PFD is a ski vest.

Some Type III vests tend to ride up when worn in the water, although adjusting the vest's shoulders and sides can help. A few models have a waist strap that helps secure the vest, and many children's models have crotch straps that will prevent the PFD from riding up.

The float coat, with built-in insulating and buoyant foam around the trunk, is another Type III PFD. Some have an attached hood, insulated arms, and a neoprene tail to lessen heat loss from the groin area. When secured, the tail also helps keep the coat from floating up around your neck. The float coat's good hypothermia protection makes it a wise choice for boating in near-coastal areas or rivers, especially in cooler climates.

Type III PFD—Flotation aid vest.

Type III PFD—Float coat with beaver tail.

Flotation coveralls (deck suits) are not considered a Type III PFD unless they are worn. See Type Vs for more information on them.

Type IV PFD—Throwable Device

Throwable devices, such as life rings, horseshoe buoys, and buoyant cushions, are classified as Type IV PFDs and have 16.5 to 32 pounds of buoyancy. Although they offer no thermal protection, some allow you to get more of your body out of the water than many other PFDs.

Keep life rings and horseshoe buoys within easy reach to throw to a person overboard. The addition of a flagpole, coil of floating line, man overboard light, and reflective tape will make it easier to spot the device and haul the person back on board.

Type IV—Horseshoe bouy.

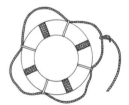

Type IV PFD—Life ring.

Type IV PFD—Bouyant cushion.

Type IV PFD—Lifesling™.

The Lifesling™ is a man overboard recovery device composed of a floating sling attached to 125' to 150' of floating line, and a container. Some versions of this are now U.S. Coast Guard–approved and can be substituted for the traditional life ring, horseshoe buoy, or buoyant cushions to meet requirements for recreational vessels.

Type V PFD—Special Use

These PFDs are approved for special use and include flotation coveralls (deck suits), work vests, and board sailing vests. They must be used according to the approval conditions on their label if they are to meet USCG PFD requirements for your vessel.

Although flotation coveralls are classed as a Type V, they qualify as a Type III when they are worn and thus meet minimum requirements for a PFD on your vessel. Although they will not keep you dry if you end up in the water, they do provide the best hypothermia protection (except for an immersion suit), especially if the waist and leg straps, and velcro around the wrists and ankles, are snug. Because of this, they are a good choice for cooler climates and seasons.

Most coveralls have an inflatable pillow that will help keep your head out of the water, but coveralls will not right an unconscious person in the water. Pillow inflation varies from suit to suit, so make sure you know how to work yours.

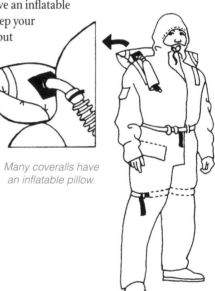

Many coveralls have an inflatable pillow.

USCG-Approved Inflatable PFDs

The U.S. Coast Guard has recently approved a series of fully inflatable PFDs that combine onboard comfort and wearability with maximum flotation when inflated. They appear in a number of types and styles, and as their name indicates, they must be inflated to work, either by mouth or from an inflation mechanism. There are many inflatable PFDs that are not USCG–approved, so read the labels and know what you are buying.

As with any inflatable PFD, it is essential to be sure that the firing mechanism works. On USCG–approved PFDs these mechanisms are required to have color coded parts so you can see at a glance whether the device is operational. Green means it is, red means it is **not** operational. Some PFDs will not inflate when there is an incompatibility between the carbon

SOSpenders™ uninflated.

SOSpenders™ inflated.

dioxide (CO_2) cartridge and firing mechanism, so **be sure** to use a cartridge suggested by the manufacturer when replacing yours. (See page 44 for replacement procedure.)

PFDS NOT APPROVED BY THE U.S. COAST GUARD

There are several PFDs that do not meet USCG specifications but may appeal to boaters.

Stormy Seas™ manufactures several models of inflatable PFDs that resemble outdoor jackets, rain jackets, and vests, each with an air bladder that can be inflated by a CO_2 cartridge or by mouth. Although they have no inherent buoyancy, they are very comfortable on board and will help keep you afloat for quick rescue.

Several companies make inflatable suspenders that can be inflated by mouth or with a CO_2 cartridge. They offer no thermal protection but, like the jackets and rain coats with inflatable bladders, they can help a conscious person stay afloat for quick rescue.

MARSARS™ makes a man overboard recovery device that some people find useful.

Stormy Seas™ jacket (Not approved by USCG).

Approved or Not Approved?

◆ The U.S. Coast Guard sets minimum standards for approved PFDs.

◆ When a PFD is USCG-approved it has met or exceeded those approved standards.

◆ PFD manufacturers choose whether or not to make USCG-approved PFDs.

◆ A PFD that is not USCG-approved may not meet the minimum standards, or it may actually exceed them.

◆ Check out your PFD label to learn more about it.

PFD MAINTENANCE

◆ Maintain your PFD as if your life depends on it—because it might. Regular maintenance prolongs your PFD's life.

◆ Avoid leaving PFDs where they will be exposed to sunlight, excessive heat, fuel or other contaminates; this can cause some PFDs to deteriorate.

◆ To prevent rot and mildew, thoroughly dry your PFDs—both inside and out—before they are stored. If they have been soaked by salt water, rinse them in fresh water before drying to help prevent metal parts from corroding. Follow the cleaning instructions on the label.

◆ After each trip, check your PFD for rips, holes, corrosion, and deteriorating fabric. Although a small tear or hole will probably not destroy the garment's flotation, it should be repaired.

◆ Lightly lubricate metal zippers according to the manufacturer's recommendation. Avoid petroleum-based greases, sprays, and waxes as they can destroy rubber and adhesives. Replace broken zippers, snaps, and fasteners.

◆ Inspect all straps to make sure they are still attached and in good condition.

◆ Try on the PFD and make sure it still fits.

- Replace any defective, peeling, or yellowed light-reflective tape.

- Some PFD manufacturers use the vegetable fiber kapok for the filling in Type I PFDs and seat cushions, sealing it in plastic bags to keep it both dry and buoyant. If these bags get punctured or burst, the PFD can lose flotation or may not float at all. If a PFD will not float itself, it certainly will not float you, so check the bags by gently squeezing the PFD, and checking to see if it resumes its manufactured shape. **If it does not, or if the PFD is waterlogged or does not float, it should not be used.** Cut it up before discarding to prevent others from using it.

- Test your PFD whistle to be sure it still works. (You aren't required to have one, but it is a good idea.)

- If you have flares in your PFD pockets, make sure they are not wet or expired.

- Look at your Type IV throwable devices to make sure they float, and inspect the attached lines.

- If you own a Lifesling™, check the tether line at the sling and where it attaches to the vessel.

- Be sure your vessel's name is clearly written on throwable Type IVs.

- Test PFD lights to make sure they work, and replace defective parts and batteries that will expire, using only batteries that are recommended by the manufacturer.

Get Your PFD Ready!

Whatever PFD you choose, it's important to adjust it so it fits, and equip it so it will be as helpful as possible. If it did not come with **reflective tape,** you can buy some at a marine store and put on your own. Some boaters have been rescued because a searcher saw light reflecting off a 4" strip of reflective tape. If you ever need to be rescued at night, you'll be glad you attached a **PFD light,** and put some **signals** and a **personal survival kit** in your PFD's pocket. (See Chapter 1, Preparing for a Safe Trip for more information on the survival kit, and Chapter 6, Signaling for Help for more information on lights and other signals.) If the PFD you want to buy doesn't have pockets, maybe you should consider another type or style.

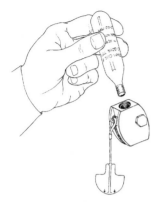

Make sure the inflator mechanism lever is up before installing a new cartridge.

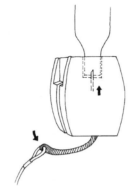

Pulling the inflator mechanism lever down pushes a pin into the CO_2 cartridge.

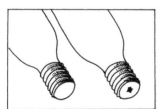

Unused (left) and used (right) CO_2 cartridges for inflating PFDs and immersion suits.

◆ Check CO_2 cartridges and replace them as needed with the exact cartridge recommended by the PFD manufacturer. Other cartridges may fit, but the firing pin might not be able to penetrate the cartridge. If this happens, the PFD will have to be inflated by mouth.

IMMERSION (SURVIVAL) SUITS

Immersion suits **(the proper name for survival suits)** have helped save hundreds of lives, largely because they provide buoyancy and considerable hypothermia protection for your five high heat loss areas. When they fit well, and are properly maintained and worn, they can actually keep you dry and extend your life by hours or even days.

Although immersion suits are more common in northern waters and on commercial vessels, they have a place in the recreational boating world, too, especially if you go on long offshore cruises. They are a good investment, and range in price from approximately $250 to $400 depending on the suit's features and manufacturer. Immersion suits do not, however, meet any of the PFD requirements for recreational boaters, so you will still need to carry other PFDs.

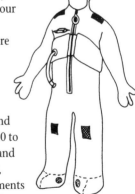

Immersion (survival) suit.

Quick Donning Technique for Immersion Suits

This technique has proven effective for boaters who need to put their suits on in a hurry in rough seas. Whatever method you use, **practice it before your emergency!**

♦ Sit down on the suit, (it's important not to stand in rough seas) and work your legs into it. **Leave your shoes on or put them in the suit with you.** You will need them on shore. Your shoes will slide in with ease if you quickly slip plastic bags over them before putting them in the suit. These bags can be stored in the suit's hood for ready access.

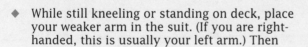
Sit down to put on your immersion suit.

♦ While still kneeling or standing on deck, place your weaker arm in the suit. (If you are right-handed, this is usually your left arm.) Then pull on your hood with your free hand. If your suit has detachable mitts, it may be easier to put your hood on after both arms are in the suit. The hood is **essential** since you lose 50% of your body's heat through your head.

Put your weaker arm in the immersion suit first.

♦ Place your stronger arm in the suit last. Pull the zipper all the way up, then secure the face flap over your face, and help others. Suits need to be fully donned for maximum protection.

♦ If you will be entering the water from a height, wait until you are in the water to blow up the flotation ring or bladder. This will help you avoid a neck or back injury, or damaged suit. See the Abandon Ship! chapter for more information.

Buoyancy

All USCG-approved immersion suits have a minimum of 22 pounds of buoyancy—not counting the air bladder—and **are constructed so the wearer will float, even if the suit is full of water.** They **will not** turn an unconscious person face up in the water.

All USCG-approved suits are required to have an attached air bladder or flotation ring that can be inflated by mouth. This will make you even more buoyant, which is especially important in rough seas.

Performance

The only way to know for sure how your suit will perform is to put it on while wearing your usual boating clothes and go in the water. Several layers of clothes underneath the suit—especially wool or polypropylene—will help keep you warm, but watch out for hats and hooded sweatshirts that can interfere with suit donning.

This is the time to decide whether to wear your glasses or secure them in a shirt pocket when you are wearing your suit. And, if you find that you can't easily grab your zipper-pull when donning the suit, use non-rotting line to secure a piece of dowel or other easily grabbed item to the pull.

When to Put Them on

Immersion suits should be donned in enough time to safely leave the boat without getting wet. Be careful—immersion suits are dangerous to don indoors on the boat, because the buoyancy can trap you inside.

Stowing Suits

◆ **Be sure your suit is stored with the zipper open!**

◆ Store your suit in a dry, accessible place where you can get to it quickly in an emergency.

◆ If your vessel carries several different sizes of immersion suits, be sure they can be easily distinguished in an emergency, especially in the dark.

◆ Designate an **exterior** location, relatively free of sharp objects, for donning suits. (Putting suits on inside the vessel can lead to mobility problems.)

IMMERSION SUIT MAINTENANCE

Proper maintenance is essential since a non-functioning zipper, bladder, or light can jeopardize your life. Visually inspect your suit and bag for rips and tears once a month, and make sure it is dry.

Shake your suit out of its bag every three months for a more thorough inspection:

◆ Examine it for rips and tears, and check the seams to make sure they are securely glued.

◆ Try the suit on, zip it up, secure the face flap, and blow up the air bladder. Check to make sure the air bladder doesn't leak, the air bladder tube is securely attached, and there are no kinks in the hose. Deflate the air bladder before storing the suit.

◆ Check the suit's light, whistle, light-reflective tape, zipper, etc. and repair or replace anything that does not work. Non-approved alterations may jeopardize the suit's USCG approval, so contact a marine supply store or your suit's manufacturer for the authorized immersion suit repair facility nearest you.

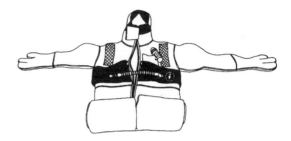

Roll your suit up with the zipper unzipped and air bladder deflated.

Avoid creases in immersion suit arms by laying the arms over the top of the rolled suit.

◆ Re-lubricate the zipper according to the manufacturer's instructions. Avoid petroleum-based greases, sprays, and waxes because they can destroy the rubber and adhesives on the zipper. Lubricate the inside of the teeth, too, and work the zipper several times, checking to make sure the zipper-pull is still securely attached.

◆ Wear the suit in the water at least once a year to check for leaks, then rinse it thoroughly in fresh water. Turn the suit inside out, dry it completely in a shady, well-ventilated place, then turn it right side out to dry the outside.

◆ **Leave the zipper open and roll the suit up**. Most manufacturers recommend rolling the suit up from bottom to top, trying to avoid any folds. Lay the arms over the rolled-up suit, put the suit back in the bag, and write the inspection date on the bag.

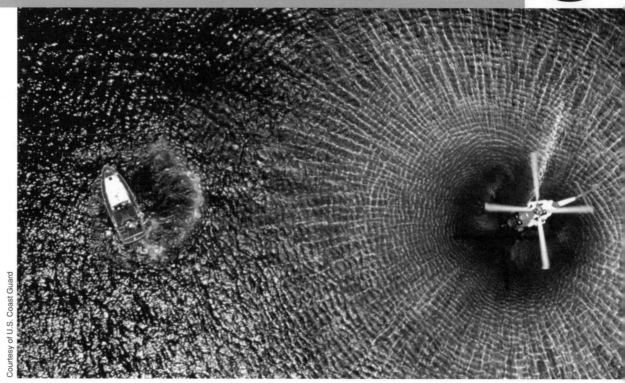

Courtesy of U.S. Coast Guard

Two men from Bethesda, Maryland, learned just how important it can be to plan for the unexpected. After their 40-foot sailboat lost its keel and capsized off the coast of North Carolina, they got into their life raft and activated their EPIRB. The EPIRB signal led rescuers to them four hours later. A few days before the trip the men had rented the raft and EPIRB from an Annapolis-based marine outfitter. As one of the men left the store he said, "I know I'll never need this."

Do you have a way to signal for help if you need to be rescued? It's hard for people to help you if they don't know you need assistance. The first step begins before you leave the harbor, and involves having a variety of emergency signals and filing a float plan.

Regardless of the size of your vessel, or whether it's designed for coastal or offshore waters or for local lakes and rivers, your emergency signals must do two things if they are going to be useful:

- **Attract attention** by being BIGGER, **brighter,** and *different*.

- **Give the message,** "Help! Help! Help!"

If your signal lacks one of these two qualities, it will not be effective.

Signals come in a wide variety of types, prices, and ranges of technology. With the right signals you might get rescued and be home before nightfall!

FLOAT PLANS

A float plan is a simple signal that costs nothing, saves time in an emergency, and can help save your life.

The U.S. Coast Guard receives many reports of overdue vessels, but the party making the report sometimes doesn't have the faintest idea where the boat was headed. If you don't know where someone is headed, it's hard to find them. The ocean is a big place, and there are a lot of rivers and lakes! When search areas are not clearly defined, rescue is often delayed or unsuccessful, and time, money, effort and lives can be wasted.

File your **float plan** in person or by mail, but make sure the person you tell will miss you and initiate a search if you fail to reach your destination on time. Your float plan should include six points of information:

1. Your vessel's name, number, and description.

2. The names of people on board.

3. Safety and survival equipment on board.

4. Where you are headed, including alternate routes.

5. When and where you expect to return to harbor.

6. Whom to contact if you fail to return.

When you return, don't forget to let your contact know. Many searches have been launched for people who were really home, but didn't tell their contact.

Example of filled in float plan.

1. Your vessel's name, number, and description.

    Get Ready, NH563491, 24' green and white Bayliner

2. The names of people on board.

    Matt, Dawn, Glenn, and Gordon

3. Safety and survival equipment on board.

    PFDs, VHF radio, flare kit

4. Where you are headed, including alternate routes.

    Lake Sunapee, launch and load at park

5. When and where you expect to return to harbor.

    Park in Sunapee, 7 p.m.

6. Who to contact if you fail to return.

    Dave Riddle, 783-6752

EMERGENCY RADIO USE

Having and using marine radios is an integral part of boating and an invaluable signal in an emergency. Two common types of radios used by recreational boaters are Very High Frequency (VHF), and Single Side Band (SSB).

VHS and SSB Radios Compared

VHF

Signal Transmission & Range
Range often up to 20 miles, but can be up to 60 miles. Signal can be bounced off repeaters so it helps to know where they are.

Comments
Common on both recreational and commercial vessels. Hand-held models can be easily taken when abandoning ship into survival craft. Waterproof and a battery life indicator are two nice features to consider for hand-held VHFs. An FCC license is no longer required for vessels less than 65 feet long operating VHF exclusively on U.S. waters.

Emergency Channel
Channel 16 (156.8 mHz)

SSB

Signal Transmission & Range
Range depends on time of day, frequency, and atmospheric conditions but can be thousands of miles.

Comments
More expensive. Requires a license by the FCC to operate.

Emergency Channel
2182 kHz
4125 kHz also monitored by USCG in Gulf of Alaska.

Emergency Calls

There are three internationally recognized radio signals used for marine emergencies: Mayday, Pan-Pan, and Security. All three have priority over other radio traffic. This information is important, so keep some paper and a pen near your radio!

Phonetic Spelling Alphabet

Radio static and background noises can make it difficult to understand radio transmissions. Many people use the phonetic spelling alphabet to spell certain words or their boat's call sign. For example, the call signs WSA 3288 for the vessel *Trinity* could be said, **"This is the Trinity, Trinity, Trinity, call sign Whiskey, Sierra, Alpha 3288."**

A	Alfa	N	November
B	Bravo	O	Oscar
C	Charlie	P	Papa
D	Delta	Q	Quebec
E	Echo	R	Romeo
F	Foxtrot	S	Sierra
G	Golf	T	Tango
H	Hotel	U	Uniform
I	India	V	Victor
J	Juliet	W	Whiskey
K	Kilo	X	X-ray
L	Lima	Y	Yankee
M	Mike	Z	Zulu

The phonetic alphabet can be very useful. Some airline reservation agents use it when confirming the spelling of names or ticket confirmation codes.

Mayday

Mayday calls have priority over all other emergency signals. **They are to be used only when a vessel or life is threatened by grave and imminent danger,** and a request is made for immediate assistance. To transmit a Mayday:

Make sure your radio is on and you transmit on channel 16 VHF or 2182 kHz SSB. (4125 kHz SSB is also monitored in the Gulf of Alaska.) Be sure your radio is **not** on scramble if it has that feature.

Then state:

1. MAYDAY, MAYDAY, MAYDAY. (Emergency signals come in threes.)

2. Your vessel's name and call sign **three** times.

3. Position (latitude and longitude if possible). If time allows, also give a geographic reference such as distance and direction from a known point. However, avoid using local nicknames that may not be familiar to others. **State your position three times.**

4. Nature of distress (fire, grounding, medical emergency, etc.).

5. Number of people on board (P.O.B.).

Listen for a response. If there is none, repeat the message until it is acknowledged or you are forced to abandon ship.

What's the most important point in a Mayday? Location, location, location!

If time allows, provide the Coast Guard with any additional information they request such as the amount and type of survival gear on board, and the vessel description. If you need to stop transmitting, say so and the Coast Guard will set up a communication schedule with you. If you are fortunate, a nearby vessel will hear your Mayday and pick you up.

Remember, it's always best to get your distress call out as early as possible. The Coast Guard would rather hear, "No further assistance needed" than "Mayday! Mayday! Mayday! We're sinking!" and the transmission ends.

Mayday Relays

If you hear a Mayday that is unanswered by search and rescue personnel you should contact the Coast Guard and relay the information to them.

Make sure your radio is on and you transmit on channel 16 VHF or 2182 kHz SSB. (4125 kHz SSB is also monitored in the Gulf of Alaska.) Be sure your radio is **not** on scramble if it has that feature.

Listen for acknowledgment, and transmit additional requested information.

Pan-Pan

Pan-Pan (pronounced pahn-pahn) calls are for **very urgent messages concerning the safety of a vessel or persons**. Examples include urgent storm warnings by an authorized station, or loss of steering or power in a shipping lane.

Warning! Wolf! Wolf! Wolf!

People have been convicted, with severe penalties, for transmitting false Maydays. Never give a false Mayday. It could cost other boaters or rescuers their life, and it may divert limited search and rescue resources from other real emergencies.

To transmit a Pan-Pan message:
Make sure your radio is on and you transmit on VHF channel 16 or 2182 kHz SSB. (4125 kHz SSB can also be used in the Gulf of Alaska.)

Then state:

1. Pan-Pan, Pan-Pan, Pan-Pan all stations.

2. Your vessel name and call sign three times.

3. Nature of urgent message.

4. Position (latitude/longitude if possible) three times.

5. Total number of people on board.

6. Vessel description (length, color, type, etc.).

Security

Security (pronounced say-cure-i-tay) calls are the lowest priority emergency calls and are used to alert vessel operators to turn to another station to receive a safety message. **Security warns nearby vessels of a possible hazard** such as a large vessel transiting a narrow channel.

CELL PHONES

Many areas of North America now have cell phone coverage, and people have been rescued offshore because they were able to dial 911, or call home on their cell phone and have their family alert search and rescue people! From many coastal areas you can be connected to the Coast Guard emergency line by dialing *CG (star CG) on your cell phone and pushing SEND. But you need to be within cell phone range for this signal to work.

EMERGENCY POSITION INDICATING RADIO BEACONS (EPIRBS)

Do you want a signal that:

- Is not affected by weather, darkness, or daylight
- Will signal for help for a minimum of 48 hours
- Has worldwide coverage
- Pinpoints your location, location, location within three miles
- Tells rescuers your vessel's type and name, and the owner's phone number?

If so, you need a 406 EPIRB!

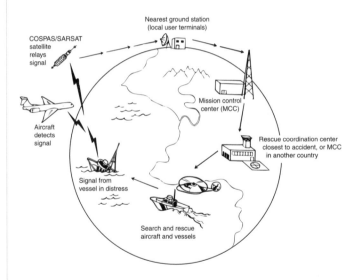

How an EPIRB signal is picked up and relayed.

EPIRBs were designed to take the search out of search and rescue (SAR). They are similar to Emergency Locator Transmitters (ELTs) carried in aircraft in that they emit a signal that can be picked up by an aircraft or satellite, and then transmitted to a land user terminal where search and rescue personnel initiate a search.

EPIRBs Compared

Category 1, 406
Frequency (mHz): 121.5, 406
Locating Accuracy (miles): 1-3
Minimum Signal Life: 48 hours at -40°C.
Self-Activated?: Yes
Will It Float Free If Vessel Sinks?: Yes
Comments: Each unit digitally coded to its owner if registration card is mailed in. Satellites can receive and hold 406 mHz signal so signal is picked up quickly. Global coverage. Some units (class 1) are designed for colder weather.

Category 2, 406
Frequency (mHz): 121.5, 406
Locating Accuracy (miles): 1-3
Minimum Signal Life: 48 hours at -40°C.
Self-Activated?: No
Will It Float Free If Vessel Sinks?: No
Comments: Each unit digitally coded to its owner if registration card is mailed in. Satellites can receive and hold 406 mHz signal so signal is picked up quickly. Global coverage. Some units (class 1) are designed for colder weather.

Class A
Frequency (mHz): 121.5, 243
Locating Accuracy (miles): 5-20
Minimum Signal Life: 48 hours at -20°C.
Self-Activated?: Yes
Will It Float Free If Vessel Sinks?: Yes
Comments: Both frequencies sent to satellite, but ground station must be in sight of satellite to relay signal. This can delay signal pickup. Coverage is not global.

Class B
Frequency (mHz): 121.5, 243
Locating Accuracy (miles): 5-20
Minimum Signal Life: 48 hours at -20°C.
Self-Activated?: No
Will It Float Free If Vessel Sinks?: No
Comments: See Class A comments. Most don't float unless wrapped in foam collar. Mini-EPIRBs can fit in a PFD pocket or abandon ship kit.

Note: 121.5 mHz is a civilian distress frequency.
243 mHz is a military distress frequency.

EPIRBs are not just for vessels far from shore; anyone who ventures away from populated cruising areas should have one on board. You can rent them, there are no confusing channel choices to make, and even the most inexperienced boater can turn on the switch that activates the device.

The newer Category 1, 406 mHz EPIRB's added power, improved frequency stability, locating accuracy, and signal holding capability gives it global coverage, something other EPIRBs do not have.

Before buying an EPIRB check out its battery life. The cost of a new battery is often one-fourth the cost of a new EPIRB.

EPIRB Mounting and Maintenance

EPIRBs are not "magic." Like any device they must be maintained and stowed properly if they are to be useful in an emergency. You've heard it before, but one of the most important things you can do is **read and follow the directions!** Most EPIRB directions are now printed right on the EPIRB.

Mounting

◆ Mount your EPIRB according to the manufacturer's instructions. Incorrect mounting can: result in it being lost overboard, cause it to fail to operate correctly, or cause your EPIRB to get snagged under an overhang or other obstruction if your vessel sinks.

If You Own a 406 EPIRB—Register It!

Each 406 mHz EPIRB is manufactured with a different coded signal, so when your EPIRB goes off, the computer reading the signal identifies it as yours. The registration card will ask for:

◆ The vessel owner's name, address, and telephone number.

◆ Alternate emergency contacts.

◆ Your vessel type, length, and call sign.

◆ Your home port.

EPIRBs are often accidentally activated when an EPIRB is moved on a boat, which is why over 90% of all EPIRB signals are false alerts. Because these "false" signals generate useless searches, most SAR units will call the skipper or harbormaster to see if the identified boat is really out of the harbor before they begin a search.

Your EPIRB registration card should be sent to:
    Registration Manager
    NOAA, NESDIS, E/SP3
    Federal Building 4, Room 0158
    Washington, D.C. 20233
    phone 1-888-212-7283 (toll free) or 1-301-457-5678
    fax: 1-301-568-8649

You will be sent a registered decal to stick on your EPIRB. (Non-406 EPIRBs cannot be registered since they have no owner identifying radio signal.)

◆ Just as with all electronic devices, it is advisable to **keep EPIRBs away from strong magnetic sources.**

◆ For Class A EPIRBs, if there is a foam spacer, make sure it is on the correct side of the battery. If you don't, your EPIRB will not float upright, and the antenna won't transmit because it will be under water!

EPIRB Maintenance

◆ EPIRBs have batteries which must be changed every three to six years. Self-activated or automatic 406 units have hydrostatic releases (the device that causes your EPIRB to automatically deploy) that must be replaced every two years. Check your manual for your EPIRB's maintenance schedule.

◆ Test your EPIRB once a month when your boat is in operation with the simple self-check that can be used to test the battery and condition of the EPIRB. (See your EPIRB manual.) It's also a good idea to log your monthly test.

Class A and B EPIRBs can be tested in the first five minutes of any hour. This is the only time this should be done, as this is the time set aside during each hour for this testing. If you do it at other times you're asking for "Help!"

If you want to hear the 121.5 signal on your class A or B EPIRB, first tune an FM radio to channel 99.5 and place the EPIRB close to the radio with the radio volume on high. Turn the

EPIRB on for **just one second or for three audible squeals.** (These squeals tell you the EPIRB is transmitting.) Then immediately stop transmitting by turning Class As on and Bs off, and properly placing your class A unit in its mounting bracket.

406 EPIRBs can be checked with just their internal test procedure. This causes the strobe light to blink at least once when the unit is tested and the EPIRB is in working order. After the test, be sure the unit is back on the ARM or Automatic setting.

◆ Check your EPIRB after rough crossings and during vessel maintenance to make sure it has not accidentally been activated. Most EPIRBs do not make any sound when they are activated, but if an EPIRB's light is blinking, it is transmitting.

EPIRB Use

◆ Be sure everyone on the vessel knows where the EPIRB is and is familiar with its operation. This should be covered during your vessel safety orientation. See Chapter 1, Preparing for a Safe Trip, for more information.

◆ Check the on/off switch whenever you leave the harbor. For most 406 EPIRBs this should be the "ready," "armed," or "automatic" setting. Your EPIRB instructions will indicate the proper setting.

◆ If an emergency occurs, turn the EPIRB on and leave it on! The batteries are designed to operate for several days in subzero temperatures. Turning the EPIRB on and off to save the battery will only hamper the search and rescue mission. There are stories from rescue personnel about nearly homing in on a signal and then having the signal disappear, because the victim turned it off.

◆ If you abandon your vessel, take your EPIRB with you! The signal will lead SAR forces to the EPIRB—and you.

◆ Try to keep the antenna vertical and as far above the water as possible.

◆ Do not let the antenna come into contact with any metal as it may short the signal.

New Technology

New technology to improve your ability to make and receive distress calls is being phased into use in the late 1990s. The Global Marine Distress and Safety System (GMDSS) will use satellite and digital technology to equip VHF radios with Digital Selective Calling (DSC) to allow you to send automatic distress alerts at a greater range than VHF radios currently do. It will also allow you to send digital calls directly to another DSC-equipped vessel much as phones work. Seriously consider buying your next VHF with built-in DSC capability or the option to have it added at a later time.

NON-RADIO SIGNALS

Non-radio signals can also be very effective.

Signal Flares

Signal flares come in a variety of types and styles, and help rescuers locate you. But flares can be dangerous and can cause damage if they are handled improperly. Become familiar with how your flares work, and beware of inexpensive, outdated, and wet flares. They have a high failure rate. Check your expiration dates and keep those flares dry!

Emergency marine signal flares include **orange** smoke, and **red** hand-held flares, meteors, and parachute flares. Within these types there are substantial differences in cost, firing mechanism, and performance.

In general, the parachute and meteor flares have the best distance visibility, hand-held flares are most useful when rescuers are in sight, and smoke flares are best seen during the day in calm weather. See the following chart for characteristics of different types of flares. **Note:** Only red and orange flares are recognized internationally as distress signals.

Flare Use

◆ Treat flares like a gun, and never point them at anyone.

◆ Turn your face away when firing the flare.

◆ Don't shoot directly at aircraft.

◆ Flares can easily start fires, so keep hand-held flares at an angle over the water, and on the downwind side.

◆ Fire one parachute signal flare as soon as possible, but keep others for when rescuers are in sight.

When firing a flare, hold the flare away from the boat, and turn your head away.

Signaling Devices

Type						
Orange Smoke	Hand-held Flare	Meteor (Aerial) Flare	Pistol-fired Meteor Flare	Rocket-propelled Parachute Flare	Signal Mirror	Dye Marker
Optimum Visibiltiy*						
3-5 miles at water level, more from the air.	3-5 miles	10-20 miles	10-40 miles	40 miles	20 miles	10 miles at 3,000 feet
Signal Duration						
50 sec. -3 min.	50 sec. -2 min.	5.5-8 seconds	5.5-30 seconds	30-60 seconds	As long as there is enough light	Dye weakens in 20-30 min. in calm seas, sooner in rough seas.
Advantages						
Compact, good for day use, can show helicopter pilots wind direction, can help locate a person overboard in daylight.	Compact, longest burning of any flare type, secondary use as a fire starter. Helps rescuers locate you. Inexpensive.	Compact, helps alert rescuers.	Easy to use, helps alert rescuers.	Most visible flare on the market for night use.	Compact, easy to use, good for day use, inexpensive.	Easy to see and carry, can also be used on snow, inexpensive.
Disadvantages						
Smoke dissipates rapidly in windy conditions, must be used in a well ventilated area, container can damage survival craft or cause personal injury, outdated containers have high failure rate.	Ash and slag can cause injury and damage survival craft, signal is low to the water, high failure rate with outdated flares.	Base triggers can get hot when flare is shot, high failure rate with outdated flares, can be difficult to operate with cold hands.	High failure rate with outdated flares, flares unusable if pistol breaks, flare can cause personal injury or damage survival craft.	Increased failure rate with outdated flares, flare may drift or be blown away from your area, flare can cause personal injury or damage survival craft.	Needs sun or other light to work, must be manned continually.	Only visible during the day, not as visible by sea as from air, dissipates rapidly in rough seas.

*Actual visibility depends on weather, altitude of rescuer, and whether it is day or night.

Signaling for Help

THE FAR SIDE By Gary Larson

"Wait! Wait! . . . Cancel that, I guess it says
'helf' "

◆ All flares are not fired the same way, so become familiar with each flare's method of firing. Although the directions are printed on the flare, it's going to be pretty hard to read them when it's dark or you've lost your contacts or glasses.

◆ Flares generally have a three year expiration date, so check the date before you buy them so you can get the maximum shelf life possible.

◆ During the recreational boating season there is an exponential increase in flare use, but many firings are not true emergencies. Boaters are often curious about how their flares work and what they look like. Drilling with pyrotechnics is very important, but there are protocols and safety measures that must be followed. This is serious stuff!

◆ Before you fire flares, **always** contact the Coast Guard, your local fire and police departments, and the FAA. (If you live where there is a lot of air traffic, the FAA is not going to be very happy if you shoot flares into air traffic lanes.)

◆ Issue a Security call on VHF channel 16 before igniting flares for non-emergency use. Include information on the type, number, time, and location where they will be fired.

Mirrors

Mirrors are a "low tech" signal that can be very effective. They can be seen over a distance of 20 miles and they can also work on overcast days. Sweep the horizon often with your mirror's signal—you may attract the attention of someone you cannot see with your naked eye. If you tie your mirror to something outside in the sun, the mirror will flash and signal without you. Mirrors can be **any** flat reflective surface, such as the back of a watch, a hologram from your credit card or even a belt buckle. Four people who had clung to PFDs for two days in the Atlantic Ocean were rescued after using credit cards to reflect sunshine to searchers!

Aiming a signal mirror.

To operate a signal mirror, position yourself with the mirror, sun, and potential rescuers in front of you. Using one hand as a sight, locate the rescuers and aim the mirror's reflected light through the sight. On a sunny day, the mirror's reflected light can be very bright, so take care not to blind potential rescuers, especially pilots.

Lights

Lights should be on all PFDs because they significantly help searchers locate you. If you are operating on crowded waterways with many navigation and shore lights, think about how you could make yourself stand out from them in an emergency. Some general considerations for lights follow:

◆ Be sure your PFD lights are watertight. Even some U.S. Coast Guard–approved lights leak water readily, but as a general rule, the more expensive the light the better its watertight integrity.

◆ If your PFD light batteries are dated they should be replaced before the expiration date; if they are not, they should be changed annually. This helps prevent corrosion, too.

◆ Strobe lights are usually brighter than regular PFD lights and are much better at attracting attention. They have saved many lives.

◆ Chemical glow sticks (personal marker lights) can be good inexpensive PFD lights, but cold water will reduce the light's intensity.

◆ Some life raft lights are operated by a water-activated battery found just below the waterline on the outside of the life raft. These batteries have an 8-hour life, but to conserve the battery you can lift it out of the water and dry it. It can then be reimmersed at night when the light will be more effective.

Whistles

A whistle is a very inexpensive way to attract attention, and can be heard three to five times farther than the human voice. The ones that depend on a moving "pea" to make noise don't work well when they're wet.

Colors

Red is usually a signal of emergency or danger. When you want to attract attention use colors that contrast with your surroundings and make you brighter and different. Fluorescent pink and orange are generally seen the best at sea. Consider these colors for your PFDs, too.

Flags

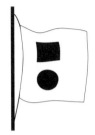

An orange flag with a black square and a black circle is an internationally recognized distress signal. Some companies are manufacturing long, red distress flags in compact cases that stream out to 40 feet. Can flags really be effective? Remember the attention the Atlanta Braves gained when they hoisted the Canadian flag upside down during the 1996 world series? (The Toronto Blue Jays won the series!)

Water Dyes

Water dyes are also available, usually in powder form, to color the water around you. They dissipate quickly in rough water, but can make you more visible from the air since they cover a large area. Although not Coast Guard–approved, they really make you look bigger, brighter, and different! Use your imagination when signaling. Rescue helicopters on Mt. Everest have landed at sites marked with Kool Aid™ in the snow.

Reflective Tape

Don't underestimate the value of light-reflective tape. Survivors have been rescued when a searcher's light reflected off the tape on their immersion suit, PFD, or life raft. Reflective tape can be purchased in strips or rolls and stuck to any equipment or clothing you wish to reflect light at night.

Other Signals

Don't forget SOS! It's an internationally recognized distress signal. And remember that "low tech" signals come in threes: 3 fires, 3 shots, 3 PFDs hanging up, etc. Use your imagination!

Get a Variety of Signals

Stock your vessel with a variety of signals that cannot be missed.

HELP! HELP! HELP!

When you are sending an emergency signal you are asking your rescuers to stop what they are doing and start saving you. Think about what signals it would take **you** to stop cruising and check something out.

Courtesy of West Marine

Let's be Frank for a moment...

One of Frank's nightmares had come true. One second he was on deck, the next he was in the water with his vessel heading out of sight in the fading daylight. Fortunately, only five or ten minutes passed before another person looked for and couldn't find him, then realized he must have fallen overboard.

Frank was rescued, largely because the people on board had practiced what to do in this situation. Once aboard, Frank was cold, wet, and embarrassed, but glad to be alive. And thankful that he had been wearing a personal flotation device (PFD)!

There is no denying it. Boaters do end up overboard. This is a serious problem and calls for quick, decisive action. You might never face this situation, but being prepared could save a life—maybe yours.

BEFORE ANYTHING HAPPENS
Devise a Retrieval System

It is **essential** that you devise a retrieval system because the sad reality is that although people overboard are often found, they sometimes die because there is no way to get them back on board the boat. There are many ways to retrieve someone out of the water, and you will need to find what works best for you and your boat.

◆ When you are practicing recovering a man overboard, be sure the smallest person can get the largest one on board, and try a rescue without help from the person in the water.

◆ In smaller vessels, there is great danger of capsizing when retrieving someone, especially over the side. Don't multiply your problems!

◆ **Do not** go overboard to assist unless you are absolutely certain **you** can be brought back on board. If you do enter the water you should be wearing a PFD, both for buoyancy and to have your hands free to help.

Lines, life rings, and throw-bags can help get the person in the water to the boat. But they are not recommended for hauling the victim back on board.

Padded slings can comfortably support a person being hoisted up onto the boat. You can easily make a homemade sling by slipping three 16" pieces of foam pipe insulation onto a line, then fashioning the line into a sling using a bowline knot. Be sure to make the loop large enough to fit over big people. For the loop, use 6 or more feet of line, and for the lifting part use line length twice your freeboard height. Add knots every 10", to help if you are pulling the person on board with brute strength.

Homemade sling.

The Lifesling™, a U.S. Coast Guard–approved Type IV PFD, is a popular and effective way to retrieve the victim and can support a person being hoisted onto the boat (see photograph p. 40.)

To hoist a victim, brute strength can do the job. It's fast and doesn't require any gear, **but** you risk hurting yourself and the person in the water. Depending on your boat, freeboard, and retrieval method, you may need to use a winch, or block and tackle to get the victim back on board.

Other techniques for bringing the victim back on board include the ladder, the elevator method, and Jason's Cradle™—a modified ladder device that can help "roll" the person in the water back on deck.

You may discover other ways to retrieve someone who is overboard. Do what works for you, the person in the water, and the conditions you find yourself in. But be prepared!

Hold Man Overboard Drills

◆ If you have never done a man overboard drill, try your first one tied up to the dock just to practice hauling someone back on board.

◆ Have a **healthy, experienced** person in an immersion suit play the part of the person in the water. (In warm water, the person can wear a PFD instead, but he should have flotation on!)

◆ A "rescue swimmer" in an immersion suit or PFD should stand by ready to assist if needed.

◆ Whatever device or combination of devices are being used, you must practice, **practice, PRACTICE!** to make this procedure as smooth and efficient as possible.

Practice Man Overboard Recovery Turns

◆ If you have never practiced recovery turns it is a good idea to use a jerry jug, buoy, or other flotation in the water (instead of a person) the first few times.

◆ There are many types of recovery turns, and people often feel strongly about which one works the best. What is important is that you know and can instinctively do at least one turn **well** for when the person is in sight, and one for when he is nowhere to be seen or the visibility is poor.

◆ In extreme wind, waves, current, and/or tide, the person overboard and the vessel will drift or be pushed away from the "splash site" at different speeds. Thus the boat and the person overboard will be in two different locations, usually with the boat downwind of the person.

Overboard!

◆ The **Simple Circle** is performed when the victim has just fallen over and is near, and the visibility is good. Turn the vessel's rudder hard over and return to the position of the person in the water. Be careful not to make a wake so large that it disorients or swamps the person in the water!

Advantages: The Simple Circle will get you back to the person in the water in the shortest amount of time. It is also a simple procedure.

Disadvantages: You may lose the person if the visibility is bad since it will not get you back to your original position.

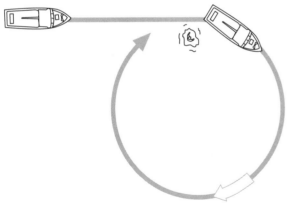

Simple circle.

◆ The **Williamson Turn** is performed by steering 60° to port or starboard off your original course, straightening out the rudder, then turning another 180° to the opposite of your original course. Your initial turn should be made to the side the person has fallen off of.

Advantages: This will bring you back on the opposite of your original course if you are looking for a person in poor visibility or if the time of the overboard incident is unknown. Follow your wake bubbles if possible.

Disadvantages: This maneuver will take longer and take you farther from the victim before you return. It is also not as easy to remember and needs practice.

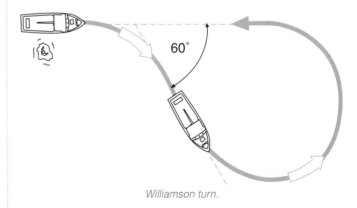

Williamson turn.

♦ The **Figure Eight** is a common sailboat maneuver. (Note: To do a successful rescue under sail, you will first have to know how to sail a boat. To learn how to sail, and to learn man-overboard procedures, taking classes at a sailing school is recommended.)

Advantages: This turn gives you time to react, no jibe is required, and the sailboat remains under control.

Disadvantages: This maneuver causes the boat to sail a long distance from the victim, and you can lose sight of him.

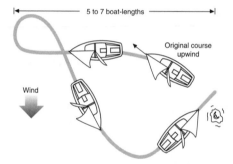

Figure eight.

♦ The **Six-Second Tack** (also known as The Fast Return) looks similar to the traditional figure eight turn when done upwind. If upwind, the boat goes to a beam reach and then tacks in a few boat lengths. If reaching/downwind, the boat heads up to a close reach and tacks. In both cases, as the boat crosses the eye of the wind, the helmsman shouts "BANG!" This helps to remind you or your crew to establish a bearing of the victim when the boat is head to wind, so you will know what point of sail is needed to head below the victim.

The boat continues to tack and leaves the jib aback, and either reaches off to drop behind the victim, or continues slightly upwind to the victim. As the boat gets close, the helmsman heads the boat into the wind and lets out the main and jib as he pulls alongside the victim.

Advantages: This is a very fast maneuver that requires no jibing. It allows you to stay close to the victim.

Disadvantages: This turn requires a crew, and is too fast for an untrained one.

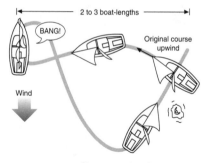

Six-second tack.

◆ **The Quick Stop** involves an immediate throwing of flotation, tacking with jib aback, and circling the victim. If crewed, drop the jib on the downwind part of the circle.

If the boat's spinnaker is flying, turn the boat immediately into the wind, and let the halyard run when the boat is head to wind. The spinnaker should mostly drop on deck. Then sail upwind to the victim. Caution: In most situations performing the quick stop maneuver will cause the mainsail to jibe in order for the boat to reach the victim.

Advantages: This is a fast maneuver that requires fewer sail adjustments and allows the boat to stay close to the victim.

Disadvantages: If the victim falls overboard while the boat is heading anywhere from a beam reach to a close-haul, a jibe will be necessary to complete the maneuver.

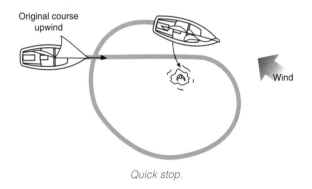

Original course upwind

Wind

Quick stop.

Again, the key to effective maneuvering in an emergency is to **practice** these techniques until they are second nature.

Crew and Vessel Preparations

In 98% of all cases, the person who fell overboard had no idea he was going to end up in the water.

◆ Prepare yourself by carefully choosing the clothes you wear on deck. Make yourself more **visible** in the event you do fall overboard by wearing bright-colored deck clothes and a PFD. Most are bright and have reflective tape on them. It's easy to add reflective tape to your PFD, rain gear, hats, and anything else that might go overboard with you. It is a very inexpensive signal. In northern climates, and on cool evenings or off season in southern climates, wear warm clothing.

◆ Whenever you are on deck, wear a PFD with a whistle and visual signaling device such as a light, strobe, mirror, and/or flares. You may also want to carry a mini-B EPIRB in your pocket to help the Coast Guard locate you.

◆ Keep "one hand for the ship and one for yourself." (Many male drowning victims are found with their zippers down since they fell overboard while relieving themselves at the rail.)

◆ Keep a throwable PFD handy—with a working light and reflective tape—to toss over as a marker in case someone does go overboard.

◆ Use a buddy system on deck after dark, especially in rough seas. Let others know when you will be outside of the cockpit.

◆ Stay sober!

◆ Where practical, have bulwarks or safety rails of adequate height, and provide hand rails alongside or on top of the cabin.

◆ Use non-skid deck coatings, and keep decks clean.

◆ Use safety lines and harnesses when doing dangerous work or in rough seas, and be sure they are strong enough. Extra stout and in good condition are watch words for this equipment since you can be thrown off balance with great force in rough seas. A person thrown several feet can generate an impact force many times his weight.

Adult body harness.

Consider what you are going to attach to when moving about the vessel. A flush, continuous line or rail will allow the carabiner on the lanyard to run freely and you will not have to unclip at any point. Otherwise, you will need two lanyards when encountering an obstacle such as a post, one to keep you attached while you clip the other one in. A line run flush on deck from fore to aft on either side of the vessel (called a dog line) can facilitate this and can be easily rigged.

◆ If you boat alone in a smaller vessel or with small children or others unable to help you in an emergency, consider installing and using a kill switch that will shut off your motor if you fall overboard. Or you may want to use a harness with a safety line that would keep you attached to the boat if you go overboard.

◆ Consider towing a skiff or knotted, floating line with a buoy on its end to provide a close target to grab or climb onto. If you use either of these methods, you **must use floating line** attached high up on the vessel, and be conscious of the possibility of the line getting fouled in the prop.

◆ Consider wearing a man-overboard alarm transmitter. These units are cigarette pack–sized and will automatically set off an alarm on the vessel if you fall overboard. The transmitter can also be manually activated by the wearer, and be rigged so it kills the engine or deactivates the autopilot, making it quite useful for the solo boater.

IF YOU GO OVERBOARD

Follow the steps beginning on page 30.

MAN OVERBOARD!
If You Are Aboard the Vessel

1. Act immediately!

◆ As soon as you know someone is in the water, you must **act immediately** and perform many tasks.

◆ The farther away a boat goes, the more likely you are to lose sight of the person in the water.

In tests performed by the Naval Academy Sailing Squadron, crews averaged 18 seconds to deploy a man overboard retrieval device. **A vessel moving at 6 knots would already be 180 feet away from the victim by this time!**

Distance Vessel Will Be from Victim

	5 knots	7 knots	10 knots
5 seconds	42 ft.	59 ft.	84 ft.
10 seconds	84 ft.	118 ft.	168 ft.
15 seconds	126 ft.	177 ft.	252 ft.
20 seconds	168 ft.	236 ft.	336 ft.

◆ **Throw something overboard to mark the person's position.** A PFD works well because it also offers the person in the water more flotation. If it is night time, turn on the PFD light before you throw it! The position can also be marked by newspaper, an ice chest, boat cushions, throwable smoke, or radar reflectors on poles (especially helpful in foggy conditions).

◆ Sound the alarm! If you can do this at the same time you throw something, great!

◆ Record the location on your global positioning system (GPS) or Loran if available.

◆ If you did not see the person go over, throw a second buoy (or something else that floats) overboard before you make the turn. This will give you two floating objects that will "point" back to the victim.

2. Post a lookout whose sole job is to keep the person in the water in sight, and to point at him.

◆ The lookout should **not** take his eyes off the person in the water for any reason.

◆ During the day, polarized sunglasses can greatly aid in spotting the person in the water.

◆ A lookout is **critical** when you consider that even one-foot seas make it difficult to see someone's head bobbing in the waves.

3. Do a recovery turn.

If the person is not in sight, retrace your path and, if it has been more than a few minutes since he was last seen, notify the Coast Guard or other vessels in your area. They may be able to assist in searching. Continue searching until you are released by the Coast Guard.

Search patterns depend on wind and sea conditions. If you have a plotter, use it. An expanding square search pattern is one that you can use to search a large area.

When approaching the person in the water, **keep the propeller away from him.**

You may decide to approach him from **his leeward side.** This does not create a lee for the person, and it might be difficult to throw a recovery device against the wind, but it may make communication easier because most people naturally float with their backs to the wind and waves.

If you do approach him this way, have him stand off until you are actually ready to bring him aboard. Otherwise, even a 1-2 foot chop will continuously beat him against the hull.

Or, you may prefer to keep him on **your leeward side,** but this can be dangerous in rough seas. Sailors may find that the flailing jib sheet has great potential to harm the person in the water when he is on the vessel's lee side. If it is not too rough, the vessel can lay to and drift to the person.

Ultimately, the approach depends on the sea conditions, your retrieval method, your vessel's maneuverability, and the victim's condition.

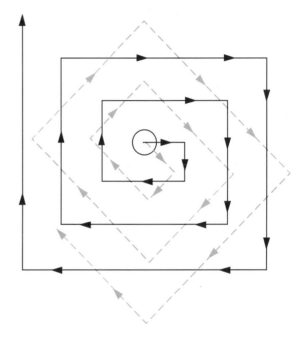

Expanding square: These patterns are started at the reported position of the most probable location of the target, and expanded outward.

4. Retrieve the person.

◆ This is often the most difficult step of all and is where practice and preparation pay off. You need some sort of man overboard recovery device and a plan to help you get the person back on board.

◆ How you retrieve the person depends on how much he is able to help, what device you are using, and how many people you have on board to help. He may be hypothermic and he will be a lot heavier due to water-soaked clothing.

◆ Put your engine in neutral to disengage the propeller. The person in the water doesn't need any more problems.

◆ Putting a person in the water to help retrieve the person overboard should be done only as a last resort. **If attempted, the in-water rescuer must be in an immersion suit (or PFD in warm waters) and attached to the vessel by a lifeline.** Otherwise you might have two people to rescue.

◆ If you are in a small boat, be careful not to tip the boat over when you are pulling someone aboard.

◆ **Talk to and encourage the person during the whole rescue. It can make a big difference!**

5. Gently treat the person for drowning, hypothermia, and other injuries as needed.

DON'T FALL OVERBOARD!

If someone falls off a dock or overboard while you are anchored up, follow these 4 steps:

◆ **Reach.** First, try to get the person out of the water by reaching with your hand, an oar, fishing pole, jacket, line, etc.

◆ **Throw.** If reaching doesn't work, throw something to him to help him float. If you tie a line to it you'll be able to pull him toward you.

◆ **Row.** If you still cannot retrieve him, row to him in a boat, or on a surfboard, air mattress, etc.

◆ **Go?** Don't go in the water unless you absolutely have to. A panicked person who thinks he is drowning might drown you.

Do all you can to keep yourself on board. It is much easier to take precautions than to hope you will get rescued if you fall overboard!

Survival Craft

K. Wynne

After their 31' sloop Auralyn was attacked by a wounded sperm whale en route to the Galapagos Islands, Maurice and Maralyn Bailey abandoned ship into their 4-man life raft. In the hour that it took their vessel to sink they transferred all their water jugs to their raft and secured their 9' dinghy to it. During their ordeal they tried to signal nearby vessels with flares several times, but were unsuccessful until the **118th** day, when they were rescued by a Korean fishing boat.

There is no doubt that having and knowing how to use a good survival craft can be essential to survival at sea. There are three types for the recreational boater to choose from: a buoyant apparatus, an inflatable buoyant apparatus, or a life raft. What you select should be determined by where you boat, the number and ages of people on board, and how soon you are likely to be rescued.

Buoyant Apparatus

A **buoyant apparatus** (BA) is a rigid flotation device designed to help support people in the water. They come in different sizes and capacities, and are designed to retain their shape and be ready for immediate use. They float either side up and have a life line attached around the outside.

One model is just a bit larger than a life ring, and it has compartments for small survival gear such as lights, flares and an EPIRB, plus attached lanyards that keep you connected to the device. (Note, however, that **buoyant apparatuses come with no standard survival equipment.**)

Buoyant apparatus— rectangular.

Others are rectangular-shaped solid platforms, or rectangular or elliptical shaped rings—with or without netting covering their hole.

Buoyant apparatuses are maintenance-free, but many are **not** large enough to keep you out of the water. Since they offer little hypothermia protection they should only be considered for use in warm waters.

Buoyant apparatus—box type.

Inflatable Buoyant Apparatus

In terms of survival, the **inflatable buoyant apparatus** (IBA) is one leap up from a buoyant apparatus. It is similar to a life raft in that it inflates and can accommodate people out of the water, but **it does not have a canopy.** Although its hypothermia protection is limited, it provides much more than a buoyant apparatus. IBAs are made in different sizes to accommodate various numbers of people, and they are suitable for near-coastal voyages in sheltered waters where rescue is not too far away.

Some IBAs are U.S. Coast Guard–approved, some are not. The CG-approved ones come in a larger container and have some survival gear. (See page 78.) Some IBAs are reversible, so you don't have to be concerned about whether or not they are right side up. Some are manufactured with ballast pockets for increased stability; others are not.

Certain manufacturers offer the choice of a soft fabric valise or a hard deck-mount container for their IBAs. The valise is intended to be stored below deck where it is easily accessible in an emergency, then taken above deck and inflated when needed. The hard container type can be mounted to float free and automatically inflate if your vessel capsizes, but you can also manually activate the inflation system.

With so many choices among manufacturers, it will pay to compare brands and features when considering an IBA.

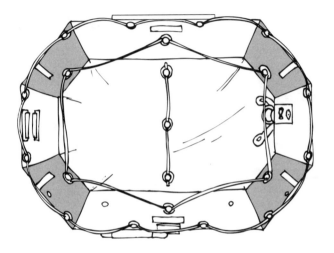

Inflatable buoyant apparatus.

Equipment Required on USCG-Approved Survival Craft

Equipment	Buoyant apparatus	Inflatable buoyant apparatus	Coastal pack for life raft	SOLAS B pack for life raft	SOLAS A pack for life raft
Quoit and heaving line	0	1 if fewer than 25 people; 2 if more than 25 people	1	1	1
Knife (buoyant safety)	0	2	1	1	1
Bailer	0	0 or 1 or 2*	1	1	1
Sponge	0	1 if fewer than 25 people 2 if more than 25 people	1	2	2
Sea anchor	0	1	1	2	2
Paddles	0	2 if fewer than 25 people 4 if more than 25 people	2	2	2
Whistle	0	0	1	1	1
Flashlight with spare batteries and bulb	0	1	1	1	1
Signal mirror	0	1	1	1	1
Survival instructions	0	0	1	1	1
Immediate action instructions	0	0	1	1	1
Repair outfit (1 set sealing clamps or plugs)	0	1	1	1	1
Pump or bellows	0	1	1	1	1

* 0 bailers required if IBA is reversible and has drains, 1 if capacity is fewer than 25 people, 2 if IBA capacity is more than 25 people.

Equipment	Buoyant apparatus	Inflatable buoyant apparatus	Coastal pack for life raft	SOLAS B pack for life raft	SOLAS A pack for life raft
Tin openers	0	0	0	0	3
First aid kit in waterproof case	0	0	0	1	1
Rocket parachute flares	0	0	0	2	4
Hand-held flares	0	0	0	3	6
Buoyant smoke signals	0	0	0	1	2
Copy of life-saving signals	0	0	0	1	1
Fishing tackle	0	0	0	0	1
Food ration	0	0	0	0	2,378 calories per person
Water	0	0	0	0	1.5 liters per person
Rustproof, graduated drinking vessel	0	0	0	0	1
Anti-seasickness pills	0	0	0	1 per person	1 per person
Seasickness bag	0	0	0	1 per person	1 per person
Thermal protective aid (a space blanket-type garment)	0	0	0	Enough for 10% of people or 2, whichever is greater	Enough for 10% of people or 2, whichever is greater

Note: The quantity of each item may change as regulations change. You can sometimes add extra things like an EPIRB, VHF radio, desalinator (water maker), glasses, prescription medications, etc. Ask your repacker.

Survival Craft Location

If you get a valise-type raft or IBA that will not be stored outside, think very carefully about where to put it. You don't want to be tripping over it (it could accidentally inflate!), but you need to be able to get to it quickly and safely in an emergency.

If you will be mounting your survival craft outside, get professional advice on the best location. The craft must be accessible and able to float free. (No lines or other gear attached to it.) Non-skid decks in the area of the craft will make it easier to launch.

Life Rafts

The next jump up is a life raft, which has some important features for survival such as:

◆ Quick, easy, convenient, and even automatic deployment. Most small rafts can be easily launched by two people.

◆ Ballast pockets and a sea anchor that help keep it stable in rough seas.

◆ A canopy to protect survivors from sun, rain, wind, or cold weather.

◆ Survival equipment that is stowed or built into the raft.

◆ The ability to prolong survival for months.

◆ An optional inflatable floor. This is an essential feature in colder climates, and one that long-term survivors in warmer waters wish they had.

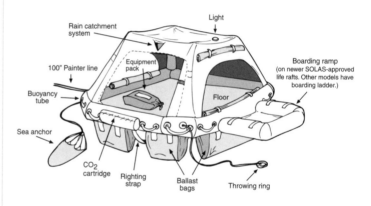

Life raft, with two doors. Cutaway shows interior.

Life rafts come in U.S. Coast Guard–approved and unapproved models. The unapproved models tend to have much less floor space, less survival equipment, and lower construction standards and quality.

What to Buy

Once you decide what type of survival craft you need, go out and buy the best one your budget can afford. Think of it as your parachute: if you need it you will be glad you bought a good one. Premium rafts often last longer and are cheaper in the long run because they need less maintenance.

Avoid buying an IBA or life raft that cannot be repacked by a convenient factory-approved repacking facility.

Life Raft/Inflatable Buoyant Apparatus Inspection

The Coast Guard says that it is a good idea to have your life raft or inflatable buoyant apparatus serviced every year by a service station authorized to work your brand. Manufacturers provide certificates to authorized repacking and service stations. Ask the repacker to show you the certificate from the manufacturer of your raft.

An annual inspection is advantageous for several reasons. Outdated flares and perishable items will be replaced, and wet rafts/IBAs can be dried out. (In wet climates water tends to work its way into canisters.) Regular inspections will greatly extend the life span of your craft. Servicing also provides an excellent opportunity to see your craft—or one of the same design—inflated. Most servicing facilities welcome the opportunity to show off their product, so take advantage of it, and familiarize yourself with its equipment. This is also a prime opportunity to ask the repacker about adding extra items to the equipment pack. Seasoned repackers have a wealth of knowledge and information.

When your raft is repacked, outdated or nearly outdated items like batteries are thrown out unless you ask for them.

Be Ready!

Get the best survival craft you can afford, know how to use it, mount or store it in the right place, and then take care of it. You might need to live in it for a long time. Just ask the Baileys.

K. Byers

Drifting for 66 days after their sailing vessel was holed by whales, Bill and Simone Butler were rescued off Costa Rica. For over two months they endured violent storms, attacks by sharks on the life raft, hunger, and depression. But in their favor was a life raft in good condition, a water desalinator, and their faith. After only a few days in the hospital, they were released. The doctors were amazed at how healthy they were after their ordeal.

Our Last Chance, by Bill and Simone Butler

Boating is a very special way to get away from it all and explore new or favorite areas, but it can also involve leaving sources of help far behind. Trouble afloat occurs all too often, and there is much to be learned from others' experiences. After all, W.P.L.F.T.M., W.P.L.F.T.M.O.O.! (Wise people learn from their mistakes, wiser people learn from the mistakes of others!)

When you carefully read survival accounts, some common themes emerge.

◆ The survivors usually had PFDs, immersion suits, or life rafts. (Shelter)

◆ They knew enough about their survival gear to make it work for them. (Knowledge)

◆ They broadcast a Mayday or transmitted an EPIRB (Emergency Position Indicating Radio Beacon) signal. (Signaled for help!)

◆ They had the will to live.

Since you don't know how **your** day is going to end, it is important to know when and how to abandon ship, and how to survive at sea.

ABANDONING SHIP

Some emergencies occur quickly with little or no warning, while others may have a delayed onset.

If you are not sure you can control a situation, contact the Coast Guard and ask them to set up a call schedule and standby. They will know something is wrong if you don't call in on schedule and will then begin a rescue.

Flooding, fire, capsizing, or grounding may someday make your vessel unsafe. Abandoning ship may become necessary, but it is a serious move. **Abandoning ship prematurely can lead to tragic consequences:**

Fifteen people perished during the 1979 Fastnet Race off England, most while abandoning their vessels into survival craft. The tragic part of this story is that most of the sailing craft that were abandoned survived the storm.

Make sure you abandon ship **only** when you are certain that being on board the vessel is more dangerous than being in the water. If you have drilled for this emergency, everyone will react much more effectively.

Once the skipper has made the decision to leave the vessel:

1. Sound the abandon ship alarm.

2. Broadcast a Mayday (see inside back cover).

3. Prepare everyone aboard.

4. Launch your survival craft.

Personal Preparations

◆ Consider wearing a hat and layers of polyester, polypropylene, wool, or other clothes that will help keep you warm even when they are wet. Even if it's hot out, that water is going to cool you off!

◆ Put on your immersion suit or other suitable PFD. If you can't wear shoes in your suit, stuff them inside it. You may need them later for protection against the sun, cold, coral, or sharp rocks. It can be difficult to escape out of a flooded compartment if you are already wearing flotation, so take care not to get trapped inside the vessel.

◆ Bring your personal survival kit, abandon ship kit (see Chapter 1), portable radio, cell phone, and/or EPIRB with you. Some of these should be in waterproof containers. This is another example of where planning ahead will make all the difference.

◆ Give yourself a clear pathway to escape, and beware of getting trapped or tangled (got a knife handy?).

LAUNCHING YOUR IBA OR LIFE RAFT

The following section refers mainly to U.S. Coast Guard–approved models:

1. If your inflatable buoyant apparatus or life raft is in a canister, free the canister from its cradle. Some models have a pelican hook that you undo; others are freed by pressing the stainless steel hydrostatic release.

2. Carry the canister (**never** roll it) or valise pack to the vessel's **lee** side. In case of a fire launch the craft away from sparks, etc. that might land on and burn it. Normally this will be the upwind side of the boat.

3. If your survival craft is in a valise pack, be sure to tie its painter off to the vessel. If you have the older style stainless steel hydrostatic release, you will need to tie your craft's painter **above** its weak link so you don't lose your craft if the weak link breaks. There is no need to tie off your survival craft if it has a correctly installed disposable hydrostatic release, such as Hammar.

4. Check to make sure there is nothing below you in the water that could cause damage, and then throw the canister overboard. (It normally takes two people to do this safely.)

5. Pull on the painter until the craft inflates. You may need to pull out over 100 feet of line and then—when you feel resistance—give a sharp tug to inflate the craft.

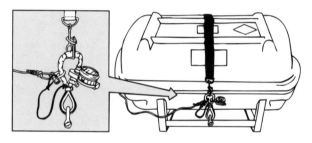

Release the pelican hook to free the life raft. Older rafts may have the type of hydrostatic release shown at right. Push the button to free the raft.

If your vessel sinks before you can remove the craft from its cradle or inflate it

A few survival craft models are designed to float free out of their cradles without any hydrostatic releases. Do you know how yours works?

If the craft has a properly set up hydrostatic release, the release will activate at a depth of approximately 15 feet and free the craft from its cradle. As the craft floats toward the surface, and the vessel continues to sink, the painter pulls out and then triggers the craft's CO_2 cartridge, and the craft inflates. Continued pressure on the craft's painter from the sinking vessel will cause the painter's weak link to part, separating the craft from the sinking vessel. Sound too good to be true? Sometimes it is. The vessel may have sunk in such a way that the raft got hung up.

If the craft is not inflated when it hits the surface

◆ Pull on the painter to trigger the CO_2 cartridge, but watch out for the bands that hold the canister together; they can pop off with considerable force. The canister halves will eventually sink.

◆ You may want to keep a screwdriver taped to the bottom of the canister in case the survival craft does not inflate and you have to pry off the canister bands. Then pull on the painter where it attaches to the wire to the CO_2 cartridge. This should inflate the craft. If it still has not inflated, find the pump in the craft's equipment pack and inflate it by hand through the deflate or topping off valves. You will need to open them first.

LEAVING THE VESSEL

◆ Abandon ship safely and **stay as dry as you can.**

◆ If you are not able to step directly into the survival craft, ease yourself into the water and use the painter to get to the craft. Jumping into or on the craft can be dangerous, especially if it is done from a height or with people aboard, so do it only as a last resort.

◆ If you must jump into the water, store your eyeglasses unless you know you can keep them on, and use the following four steps to help protect your head, neck, and groin:

What's That Hissing Noise?

You will most likely continue to hear your survival craft hiss after it is inflated. No worries, your pressure relief valves are working! Without them, the craft's CO_2 system could overinflate your raft to the point of popping. These valves should shut automatically. When you are in the raft, plug them with the craft's pressure relief valves found in the equipment pack.

1. Stand on the vessel's edge (the lee side is usually best) so you can step sideways off the vessel.

2. If you are not wearing an immersion suit:

◆ If you have a PFD on, hold onto it so it does not slip off when you go in the water.

◆ Use your other hand to cover your nose and mouth.

In the Water without a Survival Craft

This is not the best situation! As you read this, think about where your immersion suit, PFD, and survival craft are stored. Can you get to them if the vessel capsizes? You can't count on being able to go below decks. Take the time **now** to make sure they are accessible and your survival craft will float free or can be launched.

If, however, you do find yourself in the water with no survival craft it is important to know what to do.

- ◆ **Signal for help** as soon as possible.

- ◆ **Stay with the boat** as long as possible.

- ◆ **Stay afloat** with your PFD and floating debris.

- ◆ **Stay as dry as you can.**

- ◆ **Stay as still as you can.**

- ◆ **Stay as warm as you can.**

- ◆ **Stay together.** Some immersion suits come with buddy lines so you can clip to another person.

- ◆ **Don't give up!**

If you are wearing an immersion suit:

- ◆ Make sure the hood is on, it is fully zipped, and the face flap is secured.

- ◆ **Do not** blow up the suit's air bladder until you are in the water. (This prevents possible neck injuries and suit damage.)

- ◆ Put your arm that is nearest the vessel over your head, holding your elbow in, and insert the thumb on your other hand into the suit's hood. This will protect your head and permit air to escape from the suit when you hit the water.

If you must jump into the water, take precautions to protect your head, neck, and groin.

3. Look down to make sure there is no debris in the water.

4. Step off and away from the vessel, making sure your feet enter the water first!

Crossing your legs at the ankles can prevent damage to your groin area. Once you hit the water you will momentarily submerge, but will then bob up. If you cross your legs you will go farther under water.

Again, although this jumping method works, the best way is to go directly into your survival craft, or to ease yourself in the water.

RIGHTING THE LIFE RAFT

Most life rafts are not self-righting, so they can inflate right side up or upside down. If the craft inflates upside down:

◆ Find the righting strap—a nylon strap or line on the underside of the raft—and make sure you are on the **same** side as the CO_2 bottle so it won't come crashing down on your head. The newer model rafts have a notice stenciled on the bottom of the raft or pontoon that says, "RIGHT RAFT THIS SIDE" to let you know which side to work from.

◆ Pull yourself up onto the bottom of the raft with the righting strap and lean back. Be careful not to tangle your hand or arm in the righting strap.

◆ As the raft flips over, hold one hand over your head to push it off you.

◆ If you have trouble righting the raft, use the wind and waves to your advantage.

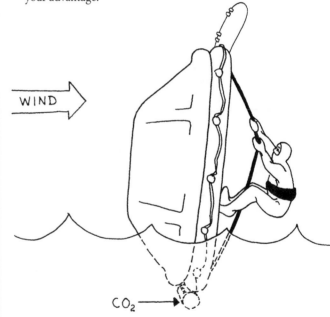

WIND

CO_2

Right the life raft by hanging on to the righting strap and leaning back.

BOARDING THE RAFT

◆ Getting into the raft from the water takes effort, especially if you are tired, cold, or injured. Some newer model SOLAS-approved rafts have an inflated boarding platform that makes entering the raft much easier.

◆ If there is no platform, locate the web boarding ladder and use your suit's buoyancy and the raft straps and ladder to your advantage.

◆ To board, grab as high onto the ladder or the raft as you can, and crouch low in the water. Then, all at once, pull yourself up with your arms, and kick with your legs. Your suit's buoyancy should help push you up out of the water. As more people board the raft it will be easier to get into.

◆ If your suit has water in it, the added weight will make you less mobile. Avoid knocking into other people when you get in the raft.

◆ Boarding a life raft is an excellent example of a skill that gets easier with practice. (If you haven't taken marine safety training that allows you to practice this skill, look in the Resources chapter for information on training agencies near you.)

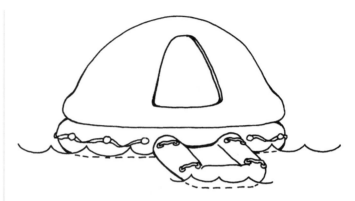

Life raft with boarding ramp.

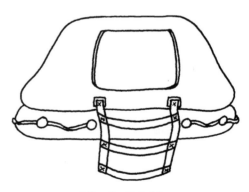

Life raft with ladder.

LIFE ABOARD THE SURVIVAL CRAFT

Once you are aboard the craft, it is a whole new survival situation. It will help to apply the Seven Steps to Survival:

1. Recognition
2. Inventory
3. Shelter
4. Signals
5. Water
6. Food
7. Play

Although the Seven Steps are listed in order of priority, you may be able to do more than one step at a time.

1. Recognition

Recognize that you are in danger!

◆ Stay tied to your vessel as long as it is safe. When you need to cut yourself free use the craft's knife, located near the door, to cut the craft's painter.

◆ In very rough seas or high winds, too many people in one part of the craft could cause it to flip, so keep the group's weight evenly distributed.

2. Inventory

As you inventory your situation, equipment, and everyone's condition, think about what can help and hurt you. This should include an assessment of the weather, tides, and currents.

◆ Provide first aid for seriously injured or hypothermic people. Less serious injuries, such as sprains or minor cuts and burns, can be treated once you have gone through the Seven Steps.

◆ Open the survival craft's equipment pack and **tie everything to the craft**—including the paddles. (See page 78 for a list of contents.) Not doing this is a common mistake among survivors, and is **always** regretted.

◆ Even the most seasoned boaters have been known to get seasick in a survival craft, so take seasickness medications as soon as possible and **before** people get seasick. Seasickness isn't only demoralizing, it is a quick way to get dehydrated.

◆ Inventory everything you have, including what people have in their pockets and immersion suits. If you have a life raft, this may be a verbal inventory until the canopy is up, the doors are closed, the raft is bailed and dried, and the floor is inflated. **Make sure sharp objects cannot puncture the craft.**

Using the mechanical patches.

◆ Inspect the craft for damage, and repair it as needed using the kit in the equipment pack.

◆ Trim the sea anchor so that when the craft is on a wave crest, the sea anchor will be digging into the trough of the wave. This will reduce your drift rate, helping to keep you near your last reported position, and will also help prevent capsizing in heavy seas.

◆ Gather up useful floating objects. Be creative, and don't throw anything away unless it will hurt you or damage the craft.

Streaming the sea anchor will slow your life raft.

3. Shelter

In cooler climates do as much as possible to conserve your body heat.

◆ Bail out the water.

◆ Top off the buoyancy tubes as needed. The CO_2 in the tubes loses volume as it cools.

◆ Empty water out of immersion suits and wring out wet clothes. (You may not be able to do this if it is too rough.)

◆ In cooler climates close the raft doors to raise its inside temperature.

◆ Put up the canopy.

◆ Inflate the floor with the air pump. (The floor is not connected to the raft's CO_2 system and must be inflated by hand.) When seas are calm, it might be necessary to have people get off the raft floor so it can be properly inflated.

◆ Inspect the craft for holes or areas of wear at least once a day, and repair or pump up the buoyancy tubes as needed.

4. Signals

◆ **Turn on the EPIRB and leave it on** until you are rescued. The EPIRB should be securely attached to the craft and placed outside, because some canopied rafts have radar-reflecting material in them that may prevent radio signals from getting through the canopy.

◆ **If you have a VHF radio, transmit a Mayday on channel 16. Call for help on your cell phone!**

◆ **Fire one parachute or meteor flare as soon as possible,** but keep others for when rescuers are in sight.

◆ Carefully **study the directions with each signal** and make sure everyone knows **how** and **when** to use each type of signal.

When firing a flare, hold the flare away from the raft, and turn your head away.

◆ **Keep other signals readily available** for use when rescuers are in sight. It may help to divide the signals into day and night types, keeping the appropriate ones near the lookout, ready to be deployed at a moment's notice. Beware that a wave may break through the door in your raft and wash out flares or other things that are not tied down.

◆ **Post a lookout** to spot ships, aircraft, land, and useful debris; to signal rescuers; and to listen for aircraft and surf. A routine of lookout watches is important to help establish a sense of being more in control of the situation and to maintain some sort of command structure.

◆ **Sweep the horizon often with your mirror's signal**—you may attract the attention of someone you cannot see with your naked eye. On a sunny day, the mirror's reflected light can be very bright, so take care not to blind potential rescuers, especially pilots. Consider tying the mirror to the outside of the raft so it can signal for help without you.

◆ **Arrange for other duties and watches like bailing, keeping the craft pumped up, etc.**

◆ Check to **make sure the raft's outside canopy light works.**

◆ **Conserve the flashlight batteries** by only using the light when it is absolutely needed.

5. Water

◆ You need a safe source of drinking water, so whenever possible **gather and store rain water**. If you are in a life raft, use its canopy collection system, if one is provided.

◆ **Decide on a daily water ration for each person.** It is now recognized that it may not be a good idea to wait 24 hours until you drink, as many manuals still state. Instead, use your body as a rationing vessel. You need fluids to do fine motor skills and for critical thinking. Odds are that you were probably dehydrated before you even abandoned your vessel!

◆ If your equipment pack has a desalinator (water maker), use it!

◆ You may be able to collect the condensation from inside the life raft's canopy.

◆ **Never** drink sea water or urine, even if your water supply is limited. They cause dehydration. Sea water has a salt content of 3.5 %, the equivalent to a full teaspoon of salt in a six-ounce glass of water. Drinking sea water exaggerates thirst and promotes water loss through the kidneys and intestines, shortening your survival time.

◆ The toxic waste products in urine add to the agony of thirst, contribute to dehydration, and lead to a body temperature of 105°F and above. Alcohol, too, promotes water loss through the skin and kidneys. (The thirst and dry feeling experienced during a hangover is from dehydration.)

6. Food

◆ Most people can live for weeks without food as long as they have water to drink. But do not eat if water is not available, unless you are eating juicy foods. Eating without drinking water accelerates dehydration.

◆ Food helps lift spirits, so if it is available, decide on food rations. Captain Bligh wrote about a method of dividing food that was time-honored even in 1789: "I divided it [a noddy, about the size of a pigeon], with its entrails, into 18 portions, and by a well-known method of the sea, of 'who shall have this' it was distributed, with the allowance of bread and water for dinner. . . . One person turns his back on the object that is to be divided; another then points separately to the portions, at each of them asking aloud, 'Who shall have this?' to which the first answers by naming somebody. This impartial method of division gives every man an equal chance of the best share."

MOTHER GOOSE AND GRIMM   **BY MIKE PETERS**

7. Play

Play is another word for the will to survive. Although this is listed as the last of the Seven Steps to Survival, it is one of the most critical steps. Survival is usually uncomfortable and painful, both physically and emotionally. But the will to survive has allowed some people to go well beyond what most of us would consider possible in a survival situation. Play is the antidote for depression. Some tips on improving morale:

◆ Keep busy and take measures to improve morale such as cleaning up.

◆ Focus on constructive ways to improve your situation.

◆ Practice "dry runs" with your signals, catch drinking water, clean up the craft, stay positive!

◆ Tell jokes. This is where practice can really make a difference.

◆ Try your luck at fishing.

◆ Your brain is your best survival tool. Be creative!

◆ Think like a survivor, not like a victim.

◆ Do not give up!

PROLONGED SEA SURVIVAL

When Nature Calls

Avoid the urge to urinate and defecate in your immersion suit; urine and feces are irritating to the skin and can cause body sores. Instead, use plastic bags and empty the contents outside the raft.

Do not be surprised if your bowel action stops because of short rations and the lack of activity. This is not unusual.

It helps to remember that thirst is not always due to water need. It can be created by sugar and salt—and even by sweetened beverages. So when water is scant, avoid such food and drink. Thirst may be reduced by chewing gum—or practically anything as long as it's not saltwater soaked—but this relief does not reduce the body's need for water.

Every bit of body water you conserve will increase the length of your survival. Much of your body's moisture is lost through breathing and sweating, so try to avoid unnecessary exertion. Ration your sweat, and save your energy until you truly need it. Don't try to paddle your raft upwind or up current.

If you are completely without water, you are apt to get delirious in about four days. If someone becomes delirious, it may take physical force to keep him aboard.

Carbon Dioxide

Recent studies show that breathing inside a battened down life raft can cause carbon dioxide levels to rise to dangerous levels. Be sure to vent the life raft occasionally to prevent this buildup.

Flipped Over

The possibility of being flipped over in a life raft may be overstated because modern rafts have much more area in their ballast pockets to maintain stability compared to older rafts. However, the risk of losing important survival gear in a capsize is real. This is a reason why survival equipment should be secured at all times. Supplies can be lost out of a raft in both calm and rough seas. **Secure all items!**

If the seas get rough and the wind howls, use human ballast to help prevent the raft from flipping. Keep your weight low in the raft, anticipate the waves and, at the proper time, shift your weight toward the waves.

If you find yourself ejected out of or tumbling inside a capsized raft, your means of righting it will depend on the sea state and number of people who can help. When a raft flips, don't get separated from it. Try to flip it right side up from the inside if possible. The people inside may be able to right it by crawling up onto the floor and using the wind to help flip it over.

With its large surface area, the life raft can easily blow away from someone trying to right it on the outside. Therefore use caution if righting from outside the raft!

PSYCHOLOGY OF SURVIVAL

Are some people more likely to survive an emergency than others? Yes! Survival is determined to a large degree by how people react to their emergency. Before discussing the actions and attitudes that lead to survival, let's cover some of the general reactions.

A small percentage of survivors—estimated to be less than 10%—feel calm during an emergency. Being calm can help you make the right moves, but being too calm can be dangerous, especially if it leads you to inaction or a failure to acknowledge the emergency.

Fear, likewise, can be healthy if it motivates you to action, but too much fear can be deadly. Panic occurs less frequently than is commonly believed, but when it does it is very contagious. It has been proven that preparation and training help decrease both fear and panic.

Initial reactions to an emergency can also include denial, and feeling numb, stunned, or bewildered. Some people may be in psychological or physical shock, while others may exhibit inappropriate behavior such as searching for a flashlight instead of taking action to rescue someone. Still others may become hyperactive, doing much but accomplishing little, even unknowingly sabotaging their survival.

During a survival situation, emotions may change from day to day or even hour to hour.

Anger—both at companions and rescuers—is a common feeling. The participants in one life raft **drill** were ready to fight after only eleven hours in a raft. In a real emergency, tempers often flare and accusations fly after unsuccessful attempts to signal rescuers. Anger is not surprising, considering the cramped, wet conditions of a life raft, but sustained anger can be deadly. A good rule is to resolve your anger before the day ends.

While some survivors experience rage, others may be totally passive and unable to help themselves. Although passivity can be a psychological reaction to the emergency, it can also be brought on by seasickness, hypothermia, injury, lack of prescribed medications, hunger, and thirst. If the cause is psychological, some people will perk up when asked to perform simple useful tasks such as bailing or keeping watch, or when directed to help an injured companion.

Some people experience guilt about what they did or did not do, especially if they think they contributed to the disaster. This can be a debilitating emotion if allowed to continue. Guilt does not help resolve the survival dilemma.

The suicidal impulse is no stranger among survivors. The person who suddenly starts over the side, saying, "I'm going down to the corner for a glass of beer," is suffering from hallucination and disassociation of time and place. It is your duty to restrain him.

Survivors tell us a great deal about why they survived. Whether their ordeal involved drifting in a life raft, being shipwrecked on land, or being held as a prisoner of war, there are common themes that run through their stories. Some of them read like headlines:

◆ ACCEPT YOUR SITUATION BUT DON'T GIVE IN TO IT.

◆ ACT LIKE A SURVIVOR, NOT LIKE A VICTIM.

◆ DON'T GIVE UP.

◆ BE POSITIVE.

◆ PRAY.

Survivors report that it is important to try to regain some sense of control over your situation, especially by acting to improve your circumstances. Schedules and routines can also help.

When you don't think you can climb back into the raft after it has flipped for the sixth time, or you don't think you can stand another day, **don't give up!** Live your ordeal one hour or one minute at a time if necessary. Remember your family and friends, and concentrate on returning home to them. Plan your future.

Be positive by talking about when, not if, you will be rescued. Of course, if you have told people where you are going and plan to be back, filed a float plan, sent a Mayday, or turned on your EPIRB, it is easier to be positive. Remember the seventh step: Play.

Many survivors describe the power of prayer in an emergency. Don't underestimate it.

Do not downplay the role your emotions can play. You can do many things to help yourself survive an emergency. Force yourself to stay on your team. Tap into your will to live!

RESCUE!

After your boat has sunk, there is hardly a more exciting sight than a vessel or aircraft headed your way. Since a survival craft or person is difficult to see from sea or air at any substantial distance, keep signaling until you are sure you have been sighted, but then stop. Don't keep firing flares at rescuers after they have located you. Most pilots and skippers take a dim view of flares fired at close range.

An aircraft will clearly show when he sees you—perhaps by "buzzing" you or dipping his wings. However, an aircraft that has spotted you may have to leave for periods of time due to weather, lack of fuel, or darkness. Sit tight and save further signals for its return. Many people become depressed after a rescue craft has sighted them, but then had to leave for some reason. Don't fall into this trap.

If you are approached by a Coast Guard helicopter, make sure all your gear stays securely lashed. Pilots don't like objects flying up into the aircraft's rotors, nor are they especially happy when someone secures the helicopter's trailing line. Would you want a survival craft tied to your flying machine?

The U.S. Coast Guard may use a rescue swimmer to assist you. These aviation survival men and women drop into the water and swim to the raft or people in the water. The chopper's nearly 100-knot rotor wash may make communication difficult, so pay close attention. You will be hoisted into the helicopter in a basket or litter.

Courtesy of U.S. Coast Guard

Keep your body—especially your hands—inside to avoid getting hurt when the basket bumps into the aircraft. One person will be hoisted at a time. If the seas are rough, this can take some time.

BEACHING

Your chance of survival is much greater on land than in the water, so if you haven't seen any potential rescuers and you are near shore, try to get there. You will need to judge the beaching situation to determine your best course of action.

As you drift toward shore, you may encounter high surf, rocks, cliffs, strong currents, and floating logs. Try to come ashore in the least hazardous area, and use the paddles in the raft's survival kit to help you through the surf. If you are in surf without a raft, try to go in feet first.

Your raft makes a great shelter and signal, so keep it if you can.

REACTIONS TO A TRAUMATIC SITUATION

After your rescue, you may find that your ordeal is still not over. Some people who survive a traumatic situation continue to feel the stress of the event long afterward. This is as true for vessel sinkings as it is for assaults, hurricanes, tornadoes, war, shootings, and other emotionally devastating events.

Common reactions may include questioning why you lived and other people died, or wondering what you could have done differently. People who experience post-traumatic stress often have flashbacks, nightmares, and difficulty sleeping. Depression, irritability, fear, mood swings, and loss of appetite are also common. All of these reactions are normal.

Once you have physically endured the experience, how can you survive it emotionally? Three things can help considerably: accept your feelings, talk to others, and try to find something positive in the experience. All three are much easier to say than do, especially if you have a difficult time dealing with emotions or talking. People who have the hardest time recovering are those who refuse to talk about what happened. It is best to talk with people who can understand how you feel and who will really listen to you. Your friends, pastor, or local mental health professional may be able to help you by listening.

Trying to find something positive in what happened may sound trite, but it helps. Some survivors buy more survival equipment and take training. Others, through their personal testimony or quiet talk, spread the word that being prepared and having the will to live increases your chances of survival.

Shore Survival

D. Brenner

Most boaters will never have to face a shore survival situation. Their ordeals occur at sea, and the majority are rescued in two or three days. But many people have boated to a remote beach to picnic, hunt or hike, only to find their boat capsized or on the rocks when they returned to the spot where they left it. In the following story some folks got stranded in another kind of mishap:

In the fall of 1989, two people sailing in Narragansett Bay on a Sunfish ended up in the water and had to swim to Dutch Island. Even though they were in a high traffic area across from Jamestown, Rhode Island, they had to spend the night on the island. When temperatures dropped to the low 50s-high 40s they took shelter in an abandoned military bunker and huddled in plastic bags. The next day they flagged down some passing boaters and were rescued.

There are many rural and wilderness areas along the North American coast where rescue might not occur so quickly. If you end up in a shore survival situation you must find ways to stay warm, signal for or get help, and gather water and food. Prioritize your actions using the Seven Steps to Survival:

SEVEN STEPS TO SURVIVAL

1. Recognition

2. Inventory

3. Shelter

4. Signals

5. Water

6. Food

7. Play

RECOGNITION

Recognize that you are in trouble! Your survival depends to a large degree on your state of mind, so think and act like a survivor.

INVENTORY

Take time to inventory your circumstances and resources, to determine what is working for and against you. Where are you and how near is help? How is the weather? Is there useful debris on the beach? What skills do you and your fellow survivors have? How is everyone's physical and emotional health?

Be creative as you think of useful items for shelter, signals, water, food, and play, and don't throw things away—you may need them later. A torn piece of plastic can become a rain jacket, part of a shelter, a water collector, or bag for food. A belt might be an essential part of a shelter, its buckle a reflective signal.

SHELTER

In cooler climates, your biggest enemy is not starvation, dehydration, or wild animals; it's the quiet killer: hypothermia, the lowering of the body's core temperature. Even in warmer climates, without proper shelter you can become hypothermic when the air temperature is below 80°F. In a hot, sunny location your shelter may be one that provides much needed shade.

Your emergency shelter may be your clothing, your PFD, immersion suit, life raft, piles of moss and leaves, or a shelter that you construct. Help yourself stay warm by keeping your head covered; you can lose 50% of your body's heat through your head. Effective shelters are weatherproof, insulated, and small.

◆ **Weatherproofing** that protects you from the sun, wind, rain, and snow is a must. The wind chill chart below shows that wind can rapidly make you feel colder than the actual air temperature by taking away the warmer air near your body. Water—whether it's fresh, salt, or from sweat—robs your body of heat 25 times faster than air of the same temperature, so get dry and stay dry.

◆ **Insulation** helps keep your body heat from escaping. The warmest shelters—including clothing—use trapped, still air for insulation.

◆ **Small** shelters trap your body heat and slow further heat loss. A large shelter may be weatherproof, but it will do a poor job retaining your body heat. If you build a shelter, make the ceiling and sides no more than six or eight inches away when you are lying down inside. If you have a tendency to get claustrophobic, you may need to make your shelter a little larger or sleep with your head near the door.

A good shelter will help keep you alive until rescuers can find you, but will they be able to see you and will they know you need help?

Wind Chill Chart

WIND SPEED (MPH)	What the thermometer actually reads											
	50	40	30	20	10	0	-10	-20	-30	-40	-50	-60
CALM	What it equals in its effect on exposed flesh											
CALM	50	40	30	20	10	0	-10	-20	-30	-40	-50	-60
5	48	37	28	16	6	-5	-15	-26	-36	-47	-57	-68
10	40	28	16	4	-9	-21	-33	-46	-58	-70	-83	-95
15	36	22	9	-5	-18	-36	-45	-58	-72	-85	-99	-102
20	32	18	4	-10	-25	-39	-53	-67	-82	-96	-110	-124
25	30	16	0	-15	-29	-44	-59	-74	-83	-104	-113	-133
30	28	13	-2	-18	-33	-48	-63	-79	-94	-109	-125	-140
35	27	11	-4	-20	-35	-49	-64	-82	-98	-113	-129	-145
40	26	10	-6	-21	-37	-53	-69	-85	-102	-116	-132	-148

Little danger if properly clothed ← → Danger of freezing exposed flesh →

☐ DANGER ▨ GREAT DANGER

Shelter Construction

If you end up on a wooded shore, and there is little time to build a proper shelter before dark, your first night might be spent in a debris bed made from a pile of moss, grass, pine needles, leaves, or branches. Make the pile as high and as weatherproof as you can, and crawl into it for protection. (Moss can hold a lot of water so it may not be a good choice in a wet situation.) Building a more permanent and warmer shelter will take several hours, so you may want to build some signals first. But do not totally ignore your shelter needs just to build signals.

Look for the natural beginnings of a shelter. You may be able to build in a cave, or next to a fallen log or overhanging cliff. When you choose a site, avoid hollows or depressions so ground water and rain won't collect in your shelter, and select a location that is protected from wind and rain, yet close to construction materials, signals, and a source of water. Balance your need to be protected from the elements with your need to be visible to rescuers.

Begin your shelter with a bed to raise you off the cold ground. Use piled-up branches, driftwood, or other materials, then lay down a two- to three-foot deep insulating layer of grass, leaves, moss, and small branches. (Remember, it will compress a lot with use.) Some sort of waterproof layer on top of the floor will help keep you warmer.

Beginning a shelter.

Once you have completed your bed, begin the structure. Use driftwood, deadfall logs, or small branches for support beams. Place them close enough to support the insulation and waterproofing layers on the ceiling and sides, and arrange all branches so the water runs off your shelter. Keep it small.

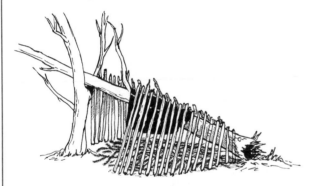

Building up the sides of a shelter.

How you insulate and waterproof your shelter depends on your materials and ingenuity. Plastic will help keep you dry (another good reason to stuff a few garbage bags in your pockets), but if it

is not available, you can use bark, large leaves, layers of branches, or perhaps some beach debris. Look inside for small holes that will let the wind, rain, and snow in and your body heat out, and plug them. If your shelter is too big, pile more branches on the bed, the sides, or on top of you.

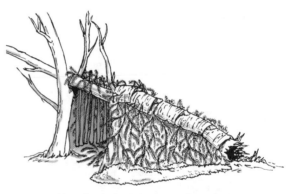

Use plastic, bark, leaves, or branches as roofing material for your shelter.

Construct a door that is weatherproof, insulated, and easily pulled into place when you are in the shelter. Make it easy to remove, too, for quick escape when you need to signal rescuers.

SIGNALS

Feeling certain they could signal one of the many passing boats, the two stranded men built a fire to attract attention. Many people saw the big blaze and talked about it, but didn't associate it with an emergency. After seeing one too many boats go by, the men scoured the beaches for crab pot buoys which they mounded into several huge piles. They then built three massive fires and stood on the beach waving makeshift flags.

People began to think something might be wrong, someone notified the Coast Guard, and the men were finally picked up. Their rescue took longer than they'd hoped because their first fire had not made it clear they wanted assistance—one bonfire looked like a beach party or a hunting camp to passing boats. Three fires in a line, mounds of orange buoys, and waving flags distinctly said, "HELP!"

Make sure signals attract and convey the need for help.

To be most effective, emergency signals must attract attention and say, "HELP!"

See Chapter 6, Signaling for Help for more information, and use your imagination!

WATER

Water is critical for survival. Most of us meet our daily water requirement of 2 to 4 quarts a day by drinking coffee, tea, milk, water, juice, and other beverages, and by eating foods high in water content such as soups and fruit.

Your best choices for water in a survival situation are rain, bottled water, and water collected from a condensation still. **Don't** drink urine, seawater, or contaminated water. The effects can be lethal.

If you must collect water from local sources, try to treat it. Although there are chemical and mechanical ways to treat water, some chemical treatments are not 100% effective, especially when the water is cold or cloudy. The most practical method in an emergency is to boil the water briskly for 3 minutes. Be sure to boil melted ice and snow, too—freezing does not kill some of the harmful organisms.

Water purifier.

Water is essential for digestion, so don't eat if you don't have water to drink. (Berries and other foods high in water are an exception to this.) When you are low on water, conserve the water in your body by avoiding excess motion and sweating.

Debris such as cans and plastic can be used for collecting rain water.

Dehydration

Dehydration can occur in any environment and can be severely incapacitating. The signs and symptoms include

◆ Being thirsty and craving cold, wet foods.

◆ Dark urine or a burning sensation while urinating.

◆ Headache.

◆ Depression or dull mental state.

◆ Lack of energy.

◆ Chapped lips and parched skin.

◆ Nausea.

◆ Constipation.

Paralytic Shellfish Poisoning

Paralytic shellfish poisoning (PSP) is a hazard found along much of coastal North America and is caused by toxins found in tiny organisms called dinoflagellates. Clams, mussels, geoducks, oysters, snails, scallops, and barnacles are all potential carriers of this potent neurotoxin.

The presence of dinoflagellates in the water sometimes causes the ocean water to turn red, which is why PSP is often called "red tide." (Red tides often contain other lethal toxins as well.) But clear water **does not** mean the shellfish is safe to eat—PSP can be present without a red tide. The time it takes clams and other bivalves to pass the toxins through their systems can be several years, not months. Contrary to what many people believe, it is **not** safe to eat shellfish in months whose names contain the letter R.

PSP can be deadly. See page 141 for information on how to treat it.

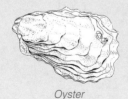

Oyster

Clam

FOOD

Food is a wonderful thing. It allows the body to repair itself and to resist infection, provides us with energy and body heat, keeps our brain functioning, and helps ward off depression. We socialize over food, sometimes plan our day around it, and spend an incredible amount of time thinking about it. Although it is important, most people can survive for up to a month or more with little or no food, which is why food is number six in the Seven Steps to Survival.

Food can often be found in abundance if you know what is edible and where to look. After his boat capsized, a man survived on Nunivak Island in Alaska for nearly two weeks before discovery and rescue. He ate kelp and year-old berries to sustain himself.

Concentrate your food gathering efforts on plants, berries, seaweed, animals in the intertidal zone, and fish. Stalking large game often expends more energy than it yields. Learn to identify edible (and poisonous!) plants and animals in the area where you will be boating. Consult the Resources section in this book, or take an edible wild foods class for more information.

PLAY

People have survived incredible disasters because they had a strong positive mental attitude. Play keeps your spirits up and strengthens your will to survive. Play means:

◆ A check-up from the neck up. Studies show that people who have a more positive attitude will maintain a higher body temperature in the cold.

◆ Staying mentally and physically busy.

◆ Improving your shelter, signals, water catchment, and cooking arrangements.

◆ Sharing stories and jokes, and emphasizing the positive.

◆ Developing a daily routine, especially for long-term survival.

◆ Continuing to act like a survivor, not like a victim.

Review the Seven Steps every time your situation changes.

FIRE

Where is fire in the Seven Steps? Although it can be an important part of your shelter, signals, water, food, and play, and can provide a psychological boost, fire is not absolutely necessary for survival. Many people have survived for weeks in the winter without a fire. What they concentrated on instead was shelter.

Giardia

Giardia, a parasite invisible to the naked eye, is found in untreated water throughout much of the world. Although many animals spread the disease through their contaminated feces, beavers are often implicated as carriers, and the disease is sometimes called beaver fever. But giardia and cryptosporidium (an organism carried by cattle, especially in the southern United States) can be carried by a number of mammals, including humans.

Signs and symptoms of giardia usually occur 10 to 14 days after drinking contaminated water, and can include severe abdominal cramps, diarrhea, vomiting, a bloated stomach, and fatigue. Because most people need prescription medication to avoid recurring bouts of giardia, it is important to avoid the illness. Don't let it complicate your survival situation.

To Build a Fire

- Fires need fuel, heat, oxygen, and the chemical chain reaction among these three elements.

- Find out what natural materials in your area really help get a fire going.

- Scrounge the beach for plastic, tires, or other material that burns well. One person's trash sometimes **is** another person's treasure.

- Use fire-starting materials in your personal survival kit!

- Building a fire takes patience. Many people add too much wood too fast and smother their fires.

- Start your fire with a spark and dry tinder, then add kindling and fuel as it gets going.

TINDER

Dry—the size of grass and pine needles.

KINDLING

Dry—twigs and small branches up to the size of your little finger.

FUEL

Larger than finger in size.

On the negative side:

- Fires can be difficult to build, especially in wet conditions.

- In order to be an effective heat source, outdoor fires need both abundant fuel and fairly constant attention.

- People have tried and failed to build fires, and then died because they neglected to build a shelter and signals.

- Fires tend to become your TV in the outdoors: once they are built, not much else gets done.

DON'T GIVE UP

Ernest Shackleton's 1914 expedition to the South Pole remains one of the most incredible survival epics, and the lessons learned from it are still relevant for today's boaters.

On December 5, 1914, Shackleton and 27 men left South Georgia Island aboard the *Endurance* and headed for a trans-continent expedition across Antarctica. By January 18, 1915, their ship was trapped in ice in the Weddell Sea. The men and the ice-bound ship drifted north for ten months until *Endurance* was crushed and sank on November 21, 1915.

"For [the next] five months the whole ship's party . . . drifted north on a huge ice . . . floe that shattered and shrank as time passed. . . . Cracks opened up under tents [and] camps had to be changed with desperate speed. . . . Shackleton displayed his superb leadership during this very trying period—keeping everyone busy, making alternative preparations for any eventualities, and maintaining morale with jokes, entertainment and special treats. . . . One evening he even cheerfully discussed taking an expedition to Alaska when the present one was finished. . . .

"On April 9 the pack ice separated and the boats were quickly launched. Then followed seven days of constant crises and danger as they jostled through the rest of the pack ice and finally out into the wild open seas to an ultimate landing on April 15 on desolate Elephant Island. . . . Nobody had any way of knowing they were there."

Shackleton's Boat Journey, F.A. Worsley, pp. 25-27.

Nine days later Shackleton and five of his men launched a 22-foot open boat in an attempt to reach help on South Georgia Island. They battled monstrous seas and poor weather for more than 800 miles until they finally landed on the southwest coast of the island—a formidable navigation feat. With three of his crew incapacitated, Shackleton and two others set off across glaciers and snowy passes in an effort to reach the whaling station on the other side of the island. No human had ever made this mountain crossing.

Meanwhile the remaining 22 men on Elephant Island faced isolation, cold, and the anxiety of wondering if they would be rescued. They had no way of knowing that Shackleton and his men had reached help until a rescue vessel came into sight on August 30, 1916, more than 19 months after *Endurance* had become trapped in the ice. Amazingly, all 28 men survived the ordeal.

Do not underestimate the will to live. People often survive what they **believe** they can survive, some in seemingly unlivable circumstances.

First Aid Afloat

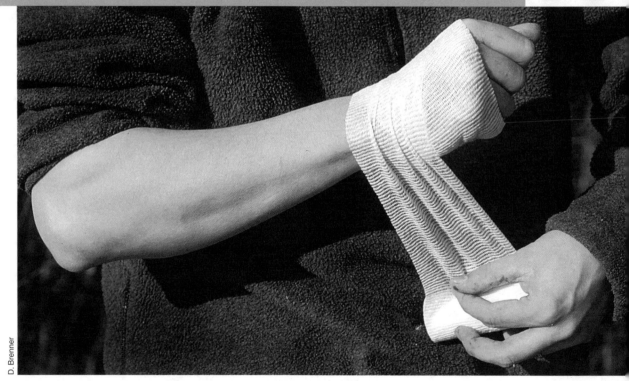

D. Brenner

The two skiffs were headed back to town on an overcast night when one slammed into an unlit day marker. The force of the impact threw one of the occupants into the marker and he sustained a serious head injury.

Would you have known what to do if you had been there? If not, this chapter is a good first step, but a first aid class would help you even more. In this chapter, life-threatening problems are discussed first. First aid concerns are then addressed in alphabetical order.

SIX STEPS FOR A LIFE-THREATENING MEDICAL EMERGENCY

1. Determine what caused the accident.
2. Be sure the scene is safe.
3. Determine if the person responds to you.
4. Check to see if the person has an airway and is breathing.
5. Check for a pulse.
6. Check for bleeding.

1. Determine what caused the accident.

◆ Look around for clues, and ask others what happened.

◆ Proper assessment of the situation can tell you a great deal about what might be wrong with the person. Someone who gets hit in the chest with a heavy object might have broken ribs, punctured lungs, breathing problems, or heart damage.

2. Be sure the scene is safe.

◆ Before you approach the victim, take a few seconds to size up the situation. Are you or others likely to be harmed from whatever injured the victim? If he is in the water, can he be recovered safely without others being harmed?

◆ You need to determine the risks to yourself before blindly rushing to assist others.

◆ If there is more than one patient, treat those with life-threatening problems first.

3. Determine if the person responds to you.

◆ If the person isn't making any noise, try to get a response by gently tapping him and asking, "Are you okay?" If he doesn't respond, he needs help!

◆ Yell for assistance if people are nearby. Contact the Coast Guard for help on the radio, or use your cell phone to dial *CG for the Coast Guard, or 911 if you are within range.

◆ Encourage the person by being positive in your speech and actions.

4. Check to see if the person has an airway and is breathing.

◆ If he is talking or screaming, he has an airway, is breathing, and has a pulse.

◆ If you are not sure if he is breathing, look, listen, and feel for about 5 seconds. You can usually do this without moving him. If he is breathing, go to step 5.

◆ If he is not breathing, you must breathe for him as follows:

If he isn't on his back, carefully turn him over, keeping the neck and back in line.

Turn the accident victim over so he is on his back.

Reproduced with permission. Textbook of Basic Life Support for Healthcare Providers, 1997. © American Heart Association.

Legal Concerns

◆ Most states have Good Samaritan acts that generally protect responders from civil liability if the patient needs immediate aid and the rescuer does not intentionally harm the patient or act recklessly.

◆ The master or person in charge of a vessel is obligated by law to render assistance that can be safely provided to any individual in danger at sea.

◆ Under U.S. federal law, some recreational vessel accidents must be reported by the vessel's operator or owner. Reports go to the proper marine law enforcement authority for the state where the accident occurred.

◆ A written report must be filed within 48 hours if a person dies or there are injuries requiring more than first aid as a result of a boating accident.

◆ A formal report must be made within 10 days for accidents involving more than $500 damage or complete loss of a vessel.

Kneel beside his head. **If the neck or spine could be injured, use the jaw-thrust maneuver to open his airway.** Put your thumbs on his cheekbones and your fingers under the corners of his jawbone and—without tipping his neck—lift the jaw up to an "underbite" position to get the tongue off the back of the throat.

If you are sure he doesn't have a neck or spine injury, use the head-tilt/chin-lift maneuver to open his airway.

Check again for about 5 seconds to see if he is breathing. If he has started breathing, go to step 5.

Use the jaw-thrust maneuver to open the airway of a victim whose neck or spine may be injured. Lift the jaw up to an "underbite" position.

If he is **not** yet breathing, breathe for him. Keep the airway open, pinch his nose shut, take a deep breath, and breathe into his mouth until his chest rises, then immediately give him a second breath. Go to step 5.

If his chest does not rise, reposition his airway, and check to make sure his nose is pinched closed and you have a tight seal around his mouth. Try to give the two breaths again. If air still won't go in, turn to the choking section on page 125.

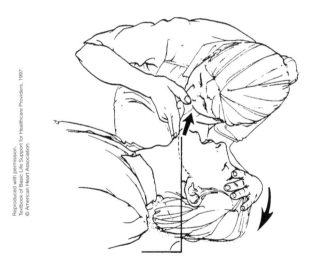

If you are sure the person does not have a neck or spine injury, use head-tilt/chin-lift method to open his airway.

5. Check for a pulse.

◆ Check for a carotid pulse for about 10 seconds. This pulse is in the neck, in the hollow between the windpipe and the large neck muscles.

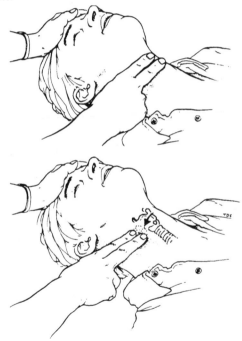

Locate and check the carotid pulse.

117

◆ Check the pulse of drowning and hypothermia victims for up to 45 seconds.

◆ If he has a pulse and is breathing, loosen any restrictive clothing, and then go to step 6 on page 119.

◆ If he has a pulse, but is not breathing, breathe for him once every 5 seconds until he breathes on his own, someone else takes over, or a doctor tells you to stop. Recheck the pulse every few minutes.

◆ If he does **not** have a pulse, do CPR (cardiopulmonary resuscitation).

Cardiopulmonary Resuscitation (CPR)

◆ If you have not contacted the Coast Guard or a physician, do so now.

◆ To find the proper hand position for CPR, follow along the bottom of his ribs until you feel the breastbone; then place the heel of your other hand two finger-widths up from the tip of the breastbone. Now put your first hand on top, making sure your hands are not on his ribs. You may need to lift or open up the person's clothing to do this.

◆ For an adult, compress the chest $1^{1}/_{2}$" - 2", then release the pressure. Do 15 of these compressions in about 10 seconds. To maintain this rate, say "1 and 2 and 3 and 4 and 5 and . . ." as you do compressions.

◆ Open his airway and give him 2 more breaths.

◆ Do 3 more sets of 15 compressions and 2 breaths, for a total of 4 sets. (Four sets should take about one minute.) Be sure your hands are in the proper position each time.

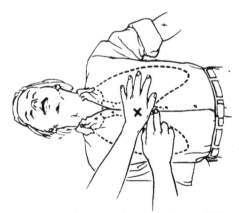

Locate the proper hand position for CPR.

◆ Check his pulse for about 5 seconds. If he has a pulse, make sure he is breathing. If he is, place him on his right side (recovery position), and be sure to check him frequently.

◆ If he does not have a pulse, continue your cycle of 15 compressions and 2 breaths, rechecking the pulse every few minutes. Continue CPR until the person breathes on his own and has a pulse, someone else takes over, you are too tired to continue, or a doctor tells you to stop. It may take you hours to revive a drowning victim.

Recovery position.

One-Rescuer CPR Standards

Age of patient	Pulse checked	For compressions use	Depth of compressions	Number of compressions to ventilations
8 and over	Carotid (neck)	Two hands	1½" to 2"	15:2
1-8 years	Carotid (neck)	One hand	1" to 1½"	5:1
Less than 1 year	Brachial (upper arm)	Two fingers	½" to 1"	5:1

CPR is very tiring, and you may become so exhausted that you have to stop. It may be appropriate to stop CPR in some situations after 60 minutes. Contact your local CPR instructor or ambulance service for current recommendations.

◆ Transport the person to a medical facility as soon as possible, continuing CPR en route.

6. Check for bleeding.

◆ Look and feel for bleeding as you quickly run your hands under and over the person.

◆ Immediately place **direct pressure** on all severely bleeding wounds, using a clean bandage or cloth. Use slightly less pressure for head wounds so you don't push broken bones into the brain.

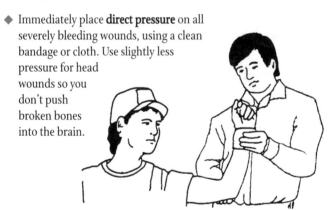

Maintain direct pressure and elevation until the bleeding stops.

◆ If the injured part is an arm or leg, **elevate it** while maintaining direct pressure. Maintain direct pressure and elevation until the bleeding has a chance to clot. This will take at least 15 to 20 minutes.

◆ If the bleeding is not controlled in 30 seconds, check to make sure you are applying pressure to the bleeding site, then resume direct pressure and elevation.

◆ If the person has a nose bleed, have him lean forward, then apply direct pressure to the nose by squeezing the middle of the nose together for at least **15 minutes.**

◆ If direct pressure and elevation do not control the bleeding on an arm or leg within one minute, use a **pressure point**—a place where an artery lies near the skin and on top of a bone—to slow blood flow to the wound. Use the brachial (upper arm) pressure point for bleeding arms, the femoral (in groin area) pressure point for bleeding legs.

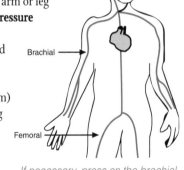

If necessary, press on the brachial pressure points when the arms are bleeding, and the femoral pressure points when the legs are bleeding.

◆ Continue to use direct pressure, elevation, and pressure points until the bleeding stops. Direct pressure can be held with a pressure bandage.

◆ Direct pressure and elevation will control most bleeding, so tourniquets are very rarely needed. When used, they often do more harm than good, and the victim usually loses the limb.

◆ If there is an **amputation**, control bleeding from the stump by direct pressure, elevation, and pressure points. Find the amputated part; keep it clean, dry, and cool (not frozen); and transport it with the person.

◆ If there is a knife, hook, or other object stuck in the wound **do not** remove it. Stabilize the object by bandaging around it. If there is an impaled object in the eye, be sure to bandage both eyes.

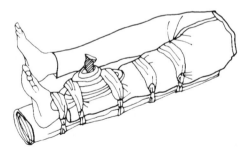

Stabilize impaled objects.

120

◆ Treat the person for shock by placing a blanket over and under him, and elevating the legs 12″. If this position causes more pain, lower the legs. Be calm, and do not give the person anything to drink or eat.

◆ Look for and treat other injuries. Contact the Coast Guard or a physician to determine further treatment.

Treat shock by elevating legs 12″.

TREATING INJURIES
Abdominal Injuries

◆ Follow the six "Medical Emergency" steps beginning on page 114, then return to this page for further instructions.

◆ Bandage wounds with a clean, dry dressing or cloth. If the person's intestines are hanging out, do not push them back in; this can cause a serious infection. Instead, cover the intestines with a clean plastic bag, or clean dressing or cloth moistened with clean water.

◆ Allow the person to lie with his knees drawn up if he prefers that position.

◆ Treat the person for shock by placing a blanket over and under him, and elevating his legs 12″. If this position causes more pain, lower his legs. Act calmly, and do not give him anything to eat or drink.

◆ Check for and treat other injuries, then contact a physician or the Coast Guard for further advice.

Burns

◆ Before approaching a person who has an electrical burn, make sure the power is off and he is not in contact with the electricity.

◆ Electrical burns usually leave a charred-looking burn both where the electricity entered and exited the person's body. Electrical burns can also cause heart attacks or internal injuries where the electricity passes through the body.

◆ Beware of breathing smoke. It can burn your airway, cause severe breathing problems, and the poisonous gases can kill you.

◆ First degree burns are red. Second degree burns are red, blistered, and quite painful. Third degree burns often look charred or leather-like. Feeling is lost in third degree burns, although the area around them may be quite painful.

◆ Stop the burning without burning yourself. If someone's clothes are on fire, stop him, have him drop to the ground, and roll. If you have a blanket or article of clothing, roll him in it.

◆ Carefully remove burned clothing and jewelry that hold heat, but do not pull on clothing that is stuck to a burned area. This should not take much time; you need to move quickly on to the next step.

◆ Follow the six "Medical Emergency" steps beginning on page 114, then return to this page for further advice. Be especially concerned about people who have facial burns; were in a smoky, closed, burning area; or who suffered an electrical burn.

◆ If it has been less than 15 minutes since the burn, the burn is first or second degree with unbroken skin, **and** the burned area is no larger than five of the patient's palms, you can cool the burn. Put it in clean, cool water—or put cloths dipped in clean, cool water on the burn—until the pain lessens. **Do not** do this to third degree burns.

◆ Bandage the burned area (including entrance and exit wounds from electrical burns) with clean, dry bandages or cloths. Also bandage between burned fingers and toes, but do not put anything else on a burn unless directed to do so by a physician.

◆ For chemicals in the eyes, hold the eyes open and rinse them gently for at least 15 minutes with clean, warm water. Flush alkali burns to the eyes (ammonia, bleach, strong detergents, lye, etc.) for at least one hour. Flush the eyes so the water drains away from the nose. This way the second eye will not become contaminated with what washes out of the first eye.

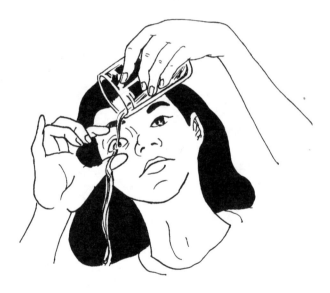

Rinse chemical-contaminated eyes carefully for at least 15 minutes with clean, warm water.

◆ For chemical burns, use a glove to brush dry chemicals such as lime off the skin, then rinse the area with clean water for at least 10 minutes. Flush alkali burns for at least one hour.

◆ Check for and treat other injuries, then contact the Coast Guard or a physician to determine further treatment. Be prepared to describe the person's condition, how the burn happened, what it looks like, and how much of the body it covers.

Carbon Monoxide Poisoning

◆ Carbon monoxide is an odorless, colorless, tasteless by-product of combustion. Because hemoglobin in your red blood cells has an affinity for carbon monoxide that is 200 times greater than for oxygen, even a small amount can concentrate quickly in your body.

◆ Carbon monoxide poisoning—and death—may occur when a combustion engine is run in an enclosed space, if your vessel has a leaky exhaust system, or if the wind is at the stern of your vessel. Air circulation around smaller vessels with cabins may cause the exhaust to cycle up toward the stern.

◆ Most carbon monoxide poisoning can be prevented by

- Using carbon monoxide detectors (they're inexpensive).
- Making sure you keep living and working spaces well-ventilated.
- Never using a cabin stove to heat the cabin.
- Not using charcoal heaters inside boats.
- Never running combustion engines inside vessels.
- Keeping your exhaust systems well-maintained.

◆ Signs and symptoms of carbon monoxide poisoning include impaired judgment, vision, manual dexterity, sense of time, and short-term memory.

◆ A headache, drowsiness, nausea, vomiting, bright red or bluish skin, and unconsciousness may also occur. Some of these symptoms are the same as seasickness, so when in doubt suspect carbon monoxide poisoning and act accordingly.

◆ Rescue the person from the area and get him into fresh air, but make sure you are not overcome by the fumes yourself!

◆ Follow the six "Medical Emergency" steps beginning on page 114, then return here for further instructions.

◆ Check for and treat other injuries.

◆ Contact the Coast Guard or a physician for further advice.

Chest Injuries

◆ Chest injuries can be caused by a blow or wound to the chest and can be life-threatening.

◆ With or without a visible wound, if a lung is punctured, the person may cough up frothy, bright red blood.

◆ Follow the six "Medical Emergency" steps beginning on page 114, then return to this page.

◆ If the person has a gunshot wound, look for the exit wound and bandage it (where the bullet went out). There may not be an exit wound—some bullets stay inside the patient.

◆ If a wound is visible where the bullet went in, cover it immediately with a piece of plastic, foil, or other airtight material. A bulky bandage or clean clothing can also be used, although airtight material works best. Tape the plastic or foil to the chest on three sides to allow air to escape from the chest cavity, but not enter it as the person breathes.

◆ Unseal the wound immediately if the person's breathing gets worse.

◆ Treat the person for shock by placing a blanket over and under him, and elevating the legs 12". If this position causes more pain, lower his legs. Act calmly, and do not give him anything to eat or drink.

◆ Check for and treat other injuries, then contact the Coast Guard or a physician for further instructions.

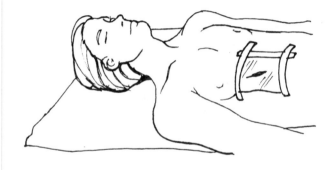

Three-sided dressing for chest injury.

Choking

◆ People who are choking often grab their throats. Some will cough while others will be unable to cough or speak.

◆ **Do not** interfere with a choking person who can breathe.

◆ If you suspect someone is choking, ask him if he can talk. If he can, encourage him to cough and do **not** leave him alone.

◆ If he cannot talk, stand behind him and place your fist on his belly between the belly button and ribs. Put your other hand on top of your first hand and—without touching his ribs—swiftly pull both in and up.

Repeat this motion until the object is out and the person can breathe again, or becomes unconscious.

Hand position for abdominal thrusts on a conscious choking victim.

If you cannot get your hands around the person's stomach, or if a woman is pregnant, do the same maneuver on the chest, making sure you are in the **middle** of the breast bone.

◆ **If the person becomes unconscious**, lay him on his back, open his mouth with the tongue-jaw lift, and sweep out any foreign objects.

Then, open the airway with the head-tilt/chin-lift maneuver and attempt to breathe for him. If the first attempt to breathe fails, then reposition his head and try again.

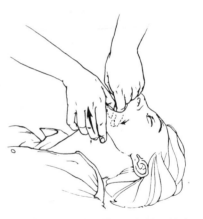

Use the tongue-jaw lift on choking victims, then sweep out foreign objects.

Reproduced with permission.
Textbook of Basic Life Support for Healthcare Providers, 1997.
© American Heart Association.

◆ If his chest rises, breathe for him every 5 seconds (checking the pulse every minute) until he breathes on his own, someone relieves you, you are too exhausted to continue, or a physician tells you to stop. If he does not have a pulse, do CPR (see page 118). If his chest does not rise, continue to the next step.

◆ If the person is very obese or pregnant, do 5 chest thrusts like in CPR (see page 118). Otherwise, straddle his legs and perform 5 abdominal thrusts.

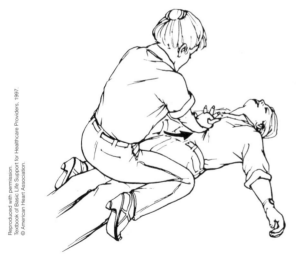

Reproduced with permission. Textbook of Basic Life Support for Healthcare Providers, 1997. © American Heart Association.

Position for abdominal thrusts on an unconscious choking victim.

◆ Then, repeat the finger sweep, breathing attempts, and abdominal or chest thrust sequence until you are successful at getting in breaths, someone takes over, or a physician tells you to stop. Once breaths go in, check for a pulse. You may need to do CPR.

◆ Contact the Coast Guard or a physician if you have not done so.

Diving Emergencies

◆ Scuba diving emergencies can be life-threatening, with the most dangerous problems being air embolism and decompression sickness. Symptoms are similar, and initial treatment is the same for these emergencies.

◆ Air embolisms occur when divers hold their breath during a rapid ascent or when air passages in the lungs become blocked. The air in the lungs expands quickly, and escapes into the space between the lungs and chest wall, the mediastinum, or the bloodstream.

◆ Decompression sickness (the bends) also develops when a diver ascends too rapidly, allowing the dissolved nitrogen in the blood to form bubbles. Because the bubbles can cause severe abdominal and joint pain, people with it often bend over, hence its name.

◆ Signs and symptoms of diving emergencies can include

- Severe chest, abdominal, muscle, or joint pain
- Respiratory and vision problems
- Dizziness, nausea, or vomiting
- Pink or bloody froth at the nose and mouth
- Skin rash
- Paralysis
- Unconsciousness

◆ A person with any of these signs and symptoms who has dived in the past 24 hours should be treated as if he has a diving emergency.

◆ If the person is still in the water, lift him out horizontally, if possible, but do not delay treatment to do this.

◆ Follow the six "Medical Emergency" steps beginning on page 114, then return to this page.

◆ Administer oxygen.

◆ Carefully remove the person's wet diving suit and cover him with dry clothing or blankets.

◆ Lay the person down on his left side.

◆ Most people with dive emergency symptoms will need further treatment in a hyperbaric chamber, so the Coast Guard or a medical facility should be contacted as soon as possible to arrange transportation.

◆ Treat other injuries as needed.

◆ Gather information about the person's dives including number, depth, time, what happened, where the tanks were filled, etc.

◆ Collect the person's diving gear, leaving it as found, and transport it with the patient to the medical facility.

◆ The patient should be transported lying on his left side in an aircraft pressurized to sea level. If sea level pressurization is not possible, the craft should fly lower than 1,000 feet.

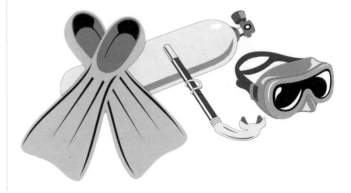

First Aid Kit

The contents of your first aid kit will depend on the type of injuries you are most likely to encounter and how far you will be from help. The items below are for a **very basic** kit for a nearshore boater; your physician or experience may suggest including other items. A waterproof container to hold the contents will serve you well.

- Pencil and waterproof paper
- Bandaids in assorted sizes
- 1" and 2" adhesive tape
- 4" x 4" sterile first aid dressings
- 2" x 10 yards gauze bandages
- 14" x 14" sterile dressings
- Triangular bandages
- Aspirin or ibuprofen
- Activated charcoal
- Syrup of ipecac
- Tweezers

- Betadine™ (or a providone-iodine solution)
- Saline solution
- Foil blankets
- Flashlight
- Needle-nose pliers
- Razor blades or a sharp knife
- Matches
- Bolt cutters
- Mouth barrier and protective gloves
- Prescription medications for infection, seasickness, etc. (Beware of allergies)

Drowning

◆ People who drown look dead. They can be cold, blue, and rigid. They will not be breathing, will not have a pulse (or will have a very slow pulse of 1-2 beats per minute), and their pupils may be dilated (big). But sometimes they may be revived!

◆ When someone has drowned, get them out of the water as soon as possible, keeping the person in a horizontal position if it does not delay rescue. Be extra careful of the back and neck if a spinal injury is suspected.

◆ Start CPR as soon as the person is out of the water (page 118). Do not do any special maneuvers to remove water from the lungs unless there is an airway obstruction.

◆ People who have been submerged under cold water **less** than one hour may actually have a chance of being revived if treated promptly. CPR is not advised, however, if the person is known to have been under water for **more** than one hour. If you are not sure how long the person has been under water, perform CPR.

◆ Contact the Coast Guard or a physician for further advice. These people need to be transported to a medical facility, even if they are successfully resuscitated, and they may need to be rewarmed in order to be resuscitated.

First Aid Training

A minimum of basic first aid training, including CPR, should be taken and kept current by at least two people who regularly go on your vessel. (What happens if only one person knows first aid and he or she gets hurt?) Advanced first aid or emergency medical technician training is even better for those going farther offshore.

When at sea, **you** are the medical emergency room. Knowing what to do (as well as what **not** to do), can make the difference between life and death in an emergency.

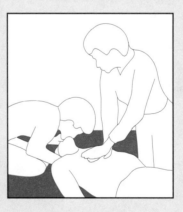

Fish Hooks

◆ Control bleeding with gentle direct pressure without removing the hook.

◆ If the hook is imbedded in the eye, ear, nose, joint, bone, genital, or other critical area, stabilize it where it is, and transport the person to a medical facility.

◆ Remove fish hooks **only** if they are surface snags or you cannot get to a medical facility within 6 to 12 hours. If you are unsure whether to remove a hook, contact a physician or the Coast Guard for medical advice.

◆ If you are going to remove the hook, **wash the area and hook** with an antiseptic solution such as Betadine™ (or providone-iodine solution) and then hot, soapy water to lessen the chance of infection, then numb the area with clean ice, and decide which hook removal method is best.

◆ To remove **surface snags**, sterilize a razor blade or sharp knife with Betadine™ or heat, then cut through the skin to the barb and remove the hook.

◆ If the hook is more deeply imbedded, use the **push and cut** method: Use needle-nose pliers to push the barb out through the skin, cut the barb off with bolt cutters, and pull the rest of the hook out in the opposite direction.

◆ The **flicker** method can also be used for small, deeply imbedded hooks, but **do not** use this method on circle hooks, as they collect too much tissue when removed this way. First, put the hooked body part on a firm surface and hold the curve of the hook with needle-nose pliers. Then, use your finger to push down on the shank of the hook to disengage the barb, and quickly pull hard on the pliers.

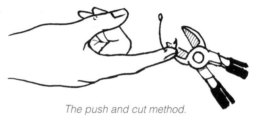

The push and cut method.

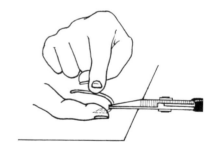

The flicker method.

◆ After the hook is removed, wash the wound with Betadine™ (or a providone-iodine solution), and then hot soapy water. Bandage the wound to reduce the chance of infection, and contact a physician for further instructions. The person may need a tetanus shot.

Fish Punctures

◆ Spine sticks from catfish, sculpin, shortspine thornyhead, spiny dogfish, sea bass, sea robin, a number of rockfish, other spiny fish, sea urchins, and stingrays can be serious, resulting in a dangerous infection or death if they are left untreated.

◆ Fish punctures can cause a painful cut or puncture, swelling, nausea, vomiting, cramps, breathing difficulties, and paralysis. There can also be numbness around the puncture wound, sometimes extending throughout the whole limb that was pierced.

◆ Extreme tenderness and a fever are signs of a spreading infection.

◆ Treat all punctures as soon as they happen. Follow the six "Medical Emergency" steps beginning on page 114, then return to this page.

◆ Carefully pull the spine straight out, making sure you get all of it, but be gentle—some spines break like glass. Save the spine so a doctor can check it for broken remnants left in the body. Some spines may need to be surgically removed.

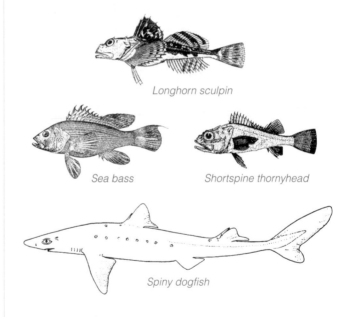

Longhorn sculpin

Sea bass

Shortspine thornyhead

Spiny dogfish

Spine punctures from spiny fish can cause serious infection or death if they are not treated.

◆ Wash the wound with Betadine™ (or a providone-iodine solution), and then hot soapy water. Then soak the wound for at least 30 minutes in water as hot as you can stand without burning yourself. The water temperature should be tested by a helper, if possible, as the injured person may not be able to judge the temperature accurately. Hand or dish soap, or Betadine™ can be added to the water. Bandage the wound and keep it clean and dry.

◆ If swelling or redness occur, soak the wound at least three times a day in hot, soapy water until the infection clears.

◆ Contact a physician or the Coast Guard if the wound becomes extremely tender, or if the patient develops a fever, numbness, or other signs of serious infection.

Fractures (Broken Bones)

◆ Most fractures are not life-threatening, but they should be considered serious until proven otherwise by a physician. Fractures to the head, neck, and back are more dangerous than others.

◆ Follow the six "Medical Emergency" steps beginning on page 114, then return to this page.

◆ If you suspect a spinal injury, go to page 142.

◆ If you suspect a head injury, go to page 134.

◆ Put a splint on suspected fractures before moving the person unless you need to act quickly because the person's life is in danger. If you need to move someone before splinting, support the fracture site and the joints above and below the fracture during the move.

◆ **Do not** pull on the arm or leg, do not try to set the bone ends, and do not push projecting bone ends into the wound. All of this may cause more injury.

◆ Check for a distal pulse (a pulse beyond the injury site) when a suspected fracture is in an arm or leg. Absence of a distal pulse is a serious condition. If it occurs, contact a physician immediately.

◆ Splint the fracture using whatever materials are handy. Try to splint the fracture in the position it is in with a **padded** splint, making sure you immobilize the fracture site and the joints above and below the fracture. This will prevent further damage.

Splint the fracture.

◆ If the person complains that the splint is too tight or if fingers or toes turn blue when the limb is splinted, loosen but do not remove the splint.

◆ Cold compresses applied to the fracture site will help reduce swelling.

◆ Check for and treat other injuries, then contact the Coast Guard or a physician for further advice.

Frostbite

◆ Frostbite, the freezing of body tissue, can often be prevented by wearing proper clothing and being prepared for the weather.

◆ Frostbitten tissue (when still frozen) looks pale or white, is hard to the touch, and has no sensation.

◆ To treat frostbite, follow the six "Medical Emergency" steps beginning on page 114, then return to this page.

◆ If the patient appears hypothermic, follow the treatment on page 138, then return to this page for thawing instructions.

◆ Do not rub the frostbitten part or put ice or snow on it.

◆ Decide whether to thaw the frozen part, but do not place the patient at risk just to keep the part frozen. Do not thaw it if you cannot do it completely or if it has a chance of refreezing. If you do not thaw the part, try to protect it from thawing and further injury, and contact the Coast Guard or a physician for further advice.

◆ Thaw frostbitten parts in moving warm water (100°-106°F) until normal color and sensation return. Then loosely bandage the part, placing bandages between thawed fingers and toes, elevate the part, and prevent it from refreezing. Try to prevent the person from walking on thawed feet.

◆ Contact the Coast Guard or a physician for further advice.

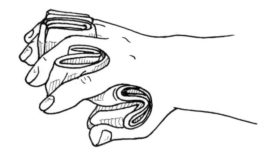

Bandage between thawed fingers and toes.

Head Injuries

◆ If a person has a head injury, **assume that he also has an associated back or neck injury**, especially if he has been knocked unconscious. Do not move the person unless you have to.

◆ People with head injuries who "see stars," lose consciousness, or don't remember what happened should be seen by a physician, even if they appear to be fine.

◆ Head injuries may be bloody, painful, and swollen. The person may have breathing or vision problems, unequal pupils, or bruising around the eyes or behind the ears.

◆ The person may also have a seizure or be unconscious. Seeing "stars," being unable to recall what happened, or being nauseous can be signs and symptoms of a severe head injury.

◆ Follow the six "Medical Emergency" steps beginning on page 114, and then return to this page.

◆ Control bleeding from the head with light pressure. Too much pressure can push bone fragments into the brain.

◆ Look for and treat other injuries, then contact the Coast Guard or a physician for further advice.

Heart Attack

◆ Heart attacks occur when the heart does not get enough oxygen and some heart muscle dies. Heart attacks can, but do not always, cause the heart to stop beating.

◆ One of the most common symptoms of heart attacks is chest pain, often described as a squeezing sensation or "like someone is standing on my chest." This pain, however, is not always present; some people have pain in the jaw or arms, especially the left arm. They may also be sweaty, have pale or bluish skin, be short of breath, vomit, or feel nauseous, faint, or dizzy. Many patients deny they are having a heart attack, while others may feel sure they are going to die.

◆ If you suspect that someone is having a heart attack, follow the six "Medical Emergency" steps beginning on page 114, then return to this page for further treatment instructions.

◆ Allow the person to sit or lie down so he is comfortable. Loosen any tight clothing, reassure him, and try to be calm.

◆ Give him oxygen, if possible, but do not let him walk or exercise. Monitor him closely.

◆ Contact the Coast Guard or a physician for further instructions, and make sure you continue to monitor the airway, breathing, and pulse.

Heat Cramps

◆ Heat cramps are caused by exercising in a hot climate without adequate salt and fluid intake.

◆ The classic symptoms are cramps in the legs and abdomen.

◆ The person should stop exercising and get out of the heat.

◆ If the person is not vomiting, have him take sips of an electrolyte-balanced fluid like Gatorade™. Or you can mix a quart of water with a pinch of salt and pinch of sugar, and have him take sips of that.

◆ Gently massage the cramps.

◆ If the heat cramps don't go away in an hour, or if the person gets worse, faints, vomits, or has convulsions, contact the Coast Guard or a physician for further advice.

Heat Exhaustion

◆ Heat exhaustion is caused when a considerable amount of body fluid is lost through sweating.

◆ Signs and symptoms can include cold, clammy, pale skin; feeling dizzy, faint, nauseous, or weak; or having a headache.

◆ A person with heat exhaustion should lie down in a cool place and have excess clothing removed.

◆ If the person is fully conscious, alert, and not vomiting, he can take sips of water or an electrolyte-balanced fluid like Gatorade™. Or you can mix a quart of water with a pinch of salt and pinch of sugar, and have him take sips of that.

◆ If there is no improvement after 30 minutes, the person should be transported to a medical facility.

Heat Stroke

◆ Heat stroke is a life-threatening emergency in which the body has lost its ability to cool itself.

◆ Symptoms can include an elevated body temperature, rapid and strong pulse, confusion, and unconsciousness. The person often—but not always—has hot, dry, flushed skin.

◆ Treatment must be prompt and aimed at rapid cooling. Remove the person from the sun or other heat source, take off his excess clothing, and spray him with cool water. The goal is to lower the body temperature to near-normal without causing hypothermia.

◆ Transport the person to a medical facility. This is a true medical emergency.

Helicopter Evacuations

◆ Helicopter evacuations are hazardous for both the patient and rescue team if the vessel has a high mast or limited deck space. High seas, gusty winds, and darkness are also hazards. Because of these risks, evacuations will be attempted only in the event of a serious injury or illness.

◆ Contact the Coast Guard if you think you need assistance. They need the following information, so gather it before contacting them:

- Vessel name, call sign, position, course, and speed

- Nature and time of injury

- Patient's name, sex, age, and country of citizenship

- Patient's pulse and breathing rate

- Amount of blood lost, other significant signs and symptoms, present medications, and treatment

- Whether the patient has any infectious diseases

- Local wind direction and speed, sea state, and cloud cover

◆ Maintain continuous radio guard on VHF channel 16, HF 2182 or 4125 KHz, or specified voice frequency. You may receive medical advice, positioning instructions, or be told to head for a rendezvous point. Advise the Coast Guard immediately if there is a change in any previously relayed information, especially the patient's condition.

◆ The air crew will discuss the most suitable hoist area with you. Pilots and crew generally prefer areas to the stern of the vessel with minimal obstructions.

◆ Because rotor wash approaches 100 mph, it is important to secure loose gear, awnings, rigging, and booms, but keep antennas up to maintain radio contact.

◆ If the hoist is at night, light the pickup area and any obstructions, but **do not** shine any lights on the helicopter or use a flash camera—they can blind the pilot. The helicopter crew will light the area.

◆ Because helicopters are noisy and voice communication will be almost impossible, it is important to prearrange a set of hand signals among the assisting crew.

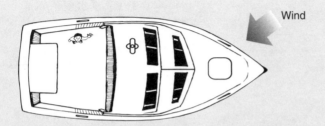

Wind

◆ Change course to permit the boat to ride as easily as possible with the relative wind 30° to 45° off the port bow. You want to find the best speed to ease the boat's motion but maintain steering.

◆ Place a PFD, plus ear and eye protection on the patient if his condition permits it. Information about the patient's condition should be in his pocket or some secure place where it will not be blown away by the rotor wash.

◆ If the patient's condition permits, move him close to the hoist area, but be alert to the dangers of rotor wash. If a litter is required, the Coast Guard will lower one.

◆ If you do not have radio contact with the helicopter, signal "come on" with your hand when you are ready for the hoist operation to begin.

◆ **To avoid static shock, allow the helicopter's basket or stretcher to touch the deck prior to handling it.** If a trail line is dropped by the helicopter, you can use it to guide the basket or stretcher to the deck. It will not shock you. Do not stand on or in front of the line and do not tie it off. The Coast Guard may cut the cable if you do.

◆ If it is necessary to take the litter away from the hoist point, unhook the hoist cable so the helicopter can haul it in. **Do not secure the cable to the vessel or attempt to move the stretcher without unhooking it.**

◆ If a basket is used, sit the patient in it, with his hands inside. If a stretcher is used, lay him in it face up and strap him in, then if cable has been unhooked, signal the helicopter to lower the cable and hook up.

◆ Signal the helicopter hoist operator when ready for the hoist: patient nods his head if he is able, and deck personnel give thumbs up. If the trail line is attached, use it to steady the stretcher or basket, keeping your feet clear of the line. Do not get between the device and the rail of the vessel.

◆ If time permits, the helicopter crew will retrieve the trail line.

Hypothermia

◆ Hypothermia occurs when the body's core temperature drops.

◆ Submersion in cold water is a major cause of hypothermia because water conducts heat away from the body 25 times faster than air of the same temperature. Hypothermia can also result from a combination of wind, cool or cold temperatures; wet clothing; or clothing that is not suitable for the weather.

◆ All water off the coast of the North America, and most inland waters, are cold enough that you can get hypothermia if you stay in them long enough.

◆ Although hypothermia can easily occur when air temperatures are above freezing, it can be prevented by using good judgment, wearing layered clothing to stay warm but not sweaty, putting on rain gear before getting wet, and avoiding being immersed in cold water.

◆ It is sometimes difficult to detect hypothermia because the affected person may not know, or may deny he is having a problem. In addition, signs and symptoms may be confused with or complicated by alcohol.

◆ Signs and symptoms of **mild hypothermia** can include controllable or uncontrollable shivering, confusion, poor coordination, and slurred or slow speech.

◆ Signs and symptoms of **severe hypothermia** can include lack of response to verbal or painful stimuli, a weak or irregular pulse, slower and shallower breathing, dilated (big) pupils, no shivering despite being cold, unconsciousness, and death.

◆ If you suspect that someone has hypothermia, check the person's pulse for up to 45 seconds when doing the steps on page 114, then return to this page for further treatment.

◆ **Do not** give alcohol to hypothermic people.

◆ Treat the person **gently.** Prevent further heat loss by carefully removing his wet clothes, covering him with dry blankets or clothes, and moving him to a warm environment, if possible.

◆ For **mild hypothermia**

- Help this person warm himself.

- If he is alert enough to get a hot drink to his mouth without spilling it, and he can swallow without choking, he can drink and eat, especially warm foods and fluids.

- Exercise will also help, as can **insulated** heat packs, and a warm bath or shower if he is alert.

Warm foods and fluids will help a victim of mild hypothermia.

◆ For **severe hypothermia**

- **No** bath or shower.

- Be gentle!

- Do not give him anything to eat or drink until he can get a warm beverage to his mouth by himself without spilling it, and he can swallow without choking.

- Transport him to a medical facility if possible. If you cannot, try to get him warm by placing **insulated** heat packs on high heat loss areas, and putting him into a sleeping bag with one or two **warm** rescuers.

◆ Make sure you check for and treat other injuries.

◆ Contact the Coast Guard or a physician for further advice.

Infections from Handling Fish

◆ Infections from handling fish, sometimes called fish poisoning, can develop when bacteria from the fish enters your body through cuts, scrapes, or punctures. If you do a lot of fishing, you can prevent most fish poisoning by keeping your hands clean and dry, and washing your hands with Betadine™ (or a providone-iodine solution) and then hot soapy water at least twice a day.

◆ Antibiotics such as Keflex™ or erythromycin are commonly prescribed for fish poisoning, so if you travel far from your harbor, consider asking your doctor for a prescription for an antibiotic to keep on board in case someone gets fish poisoning.

◆ Swelling and redness at the wound site are common signs of fish poisoning, and can increase as the infection spreads. A fever or chills may also develop with a worsening infection.

◆ Wash wounds with Betadine™, and then hot, soapy water as soon as they occur. Then dry and bandage the wounds.

◆ If the wound looks infected, soak it for a half-hour in hot, soapy water at least three times a day (use dish soap in water as hot as you can stand without burning yourself). Then dry and bandage the wound.

◆ Some doctors recommend wrapping a wet, room-temperature tea bag around the wound for 10 minutes several times a day. Use regular tea bags, not herbal, and then dry and bandage the wound.

◆ Contact your doctor or the Coast Guard if the infection gets worse or does not clear up in a few days. In very severe cases, surgery may be necessary to drain the pus from the infection.

Jellyfish Stings

◆ Jellyfish and Portuguese man-of-war stings are treated differently. See page 141 for treatment for Portuguese man-of-war stings.

◆ Jellyfish stings occur when the stinging cells on the jellyfish's tentacles touch your skin, then release a poison that can cause a temporary burning pain and skin rash. In serious cases, the stings may cause cramps, difficulty breathing, shock, nausea, or vomiting.

◆ Do a quick airway, breathing, and circulation check by following the six "Medical Emergency" steps beginning on page 114, then return to this page.

◆ If tentacles are in the eyes, rinse eyes with copious amounts of room temperature water for at least 15 minutes. Do **not** use vinegar or other remedies in the eyes. If pain, redness, swelling, or other problems persist, contact a physician.

◆ If the tentacles are **not** in the eyes, pour vinegar on the site to help prevent the stinging cells from firing, then remove the tentacles with a cloth or stick (**not** your hands!).

◆ Ice packs may help control pain.

◆ In severe cases, contact the Coast Guard or a doctor for further advice.

Neck Injuries

◆ See treatment for spinal injuries on page 142.

Paralytic Shellfish Poisoning

◆ Paralytic shellfish poisoning (PSP) results when people consume shellfish that has eaten small organisms containing a toxin which is 1,000 times more toxic than cyanide.

◆ Signs and symptoms of PSP usually occur within 10 to 30 minutes after eating affected seafood. Problems can include nausea, vomiting, diarrhea, and abdominal pain. The person may also have tingling or burning lips, gums, tongue, face, neck, arms, legs, or toes.

◆ Later problems may include shortness of breath, dry mouth, a choking feeling, confused or slurred speech, and lack of coordination.

◆ Start treatment by following the "Medical Emergency" steps beginning on page 114, then return to this page. Respiratory difficulties are usually what kill people with PSP, so be prepared for them.

◆ Contact the Coast Guard or a physician for further advice.

Portuguese Man-of-War Stings

◆ The treatment for jellyfish stings is a bit different from Portuguese man-of-war stings. See page 140 for treatment for jellyfish stings.

◆ Portuguese man-of-war stings occur when the stinging cells on its tentacles touch your skin, then release a poison that can cause severe pain. In serious cases, the stings may cause cramps, difficulty breathing, shock, nausea, or vomiting.

Portuguese man-of-war.   *Jellyfish.*

◆ Do a quick airway, breathing, and circulation check by following the six "Medical Emergency" steps beginning on page 114, then return to this page.

◆ Pick off tentacles with a stick or other tool (**not** your hands!), being careful to avoid injuring the patient or yourself.

◆ If tentacles are in the eyes, rinse them with a clean saline solution (or clean seawater— without jellyfish—if saline is not available) until the burning stops. **Do not** use fresh water, this will cause the stinging cells to fire.

◆ If the tentacles are **not** in the eyes, pour seawater or fresh water on the site to remove other stinging cells. (Vinegar is no longer recommended for Portuguese man-of-war sting treatment.)

◆ Ice may be used to help control pain.

◆ In severe cases, contact the Coast Guard or a doctor for further advice.

Seizures

◆ Seizures result from a massive electrical discharge in the brain caused by epilepsy, old or recent head injuries, alcohol withdrawal, diabetic problems, poisoning, fever, drugs, and low levels of oxygen in the brain.

◆ Seizures are often accompanied by convulsions (involuntary body movements).

◆ When someone is having a seizure, **do not** try to restrain him, and **do not** put anything in his mouth. Protect the person by clearing the area of sharp objects or items he might knock onto himself.

◆ Contact the Coast Guard or a physician immediately if a person has one seizure after another. This is a serious emergency.

◆ When the seizure is over, follow the six "Medical Emergency" steps beginning on page 114, then return to this page.

◆ Look for and treat other injuries, then contact the Coast Guard or a physician for further instructions.

Spinal Injuries

◆ **If there is a chance the person has a spinal injury because of the type of accident, treat him as if he does.**

◆ If a person is unconscious for an unknown reason, has a head or neck injury, or injury above mid-chest, treat him as if he has a spinal injury.

◆ Signs and symptoms of spinal injuries may include a wound, pain at the site, numbness, tingling, lack of feeling, or inability to move the body below the injury site. But it is also possible for a person to have a spinal injury and show none of these signs or symptoms.

◆ Follow the six "Medical Emergency" steps beginning on page 114, being sure to open the person's airway, if needed, with the jaw-thrust maneuver; then return to this page.

◆ Look for and treat other injuries before moving the patient. Do not move him until you have enough people and the proper equipment; improper handling can paralyze a person for life.

◆ If you must move the person, **do not bend his neck or spine.** Put a blanket on a backboard, door, or other firm, large object and then place him on it in the position he is in. Then, cover him and secure him to the board so he will not move or shift when the board is moved.

◆ Contact the Coast Guard or a physician for further medical advice.

Stroke

◆ Strokes (sometimes called brain attacks) occur when blood flow is blocked to a portion of the brain, or when a blood vessel ruptures in the brain.

◆ Signs and symptoms may have a slow or rapid onset. The person may have unequal pupils, a severe headache, or be dizzy or unconscious.

◆ He may also have trouble seeing, moving, talking, swallowing, or thinking. Some experience paralysis on one or both sides of their bodies.

◆ Follow the six "Medical Emergency" steps beginning on page 114.

◆ Be gentle, but seek immediate transport to a medical facility, if possible. Prompt hospital care has been shown to reduce or diminish the effects of some strokes.

Courtesy of U.S. Coast Guard

A Sitka couple on a weekend outing suffered burns to hands and faces, and spent a night on the beach after their boat caught fire and burned to the waterline. They were at anchor in their 24-foot Bayliner at 8:30 p.m. "All of a sudden I saw this wall of flame," said Darold Betts. "I told Diane to get out of there. The whole inside was engulfed in just a couple of seconds."

Daily Sitka Sentinel, Sitka, Alaska

Fires on vessels are frightening and can very quickly overcome most boats' scant fire-fighting resources. This chapter will help you understand the different types of fires, how to use extinguishers, how to fight fires, and most important, the fire prevention steps to take on your vessel. Remember, when you leave the dock, **you** are the fire department!

FIRE

In order to burn, a fire must have fuel, heat, and oxygen—plus the chemical chain reaction between these components.

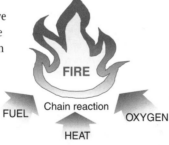

TYPES OF FIRES

Fuel for fires can be provided by anything as long as there is enough heat to vaporize it into gas, which is what burns in a fire. This explains why gasoline and other petroleum liquids are so dangerous—they vaporize at low temperatures.

Fires are categorized into four classes—A, B, C, or D—depending on the fuel.

Fires often become a combination of several classes. An engine room fire would most likely be a BC fire, but could easily develop into an ABC fire.

Class of Fire Depends on Type of Fuel

Class of Fire	Fueled by
A	Wood, bedding, clothing, canvas, rope, and paper. They leave an **ash** when they burn.
B	Flammable or combustible liquids such as gasoline, oil, paint, grease, etc., some plastic, and flammable or combustible gases such as acetylene and propane. Most class B fires **boil**.
C	Electrical fires are ignited by electric **current** and involve some other fuel.
D	Caused by **combustible metals** like in emergency flares.

How Extinguishing Agents Put out Fires

Extingushing Agent	How it works	Comments
Water	Cools the fire.	Readily available, but can ruin electronics and make vessel unstable. Spraying water onto anything electrical can conduct the electricity to you and kill you.
Carbon dioxide (CO_2)	It is 1½ times heavier than air, so it deprives the fire of oxygen.	Leaves no residue. Heavy extinguisher with short (3'-8') shooting range. Does not work well in wind. May damage electronic equipment by thermal shock. Avoid static spark by grounding extinguisher to deck while applying agent. Avoid touching metal nozzle; it gets so cold it can give you frostbite. Very dangerous to breathe.
Foam	Cools the fire and deprives it of oxygen.	Foam is 97% water and can shock you when used on electrical fires. Can ruin electronics. Subject to freezing.
Dry chemical	Interferes with the chemical reaction.	Often ruins electronic equipment. Makes a mess and causes corrosion.
Halon	Interferes with the chemical reaction. Removes enough heat to bring the material below the ignition point.	Works more quickly than CO_2 and reduces number of fire reflashes. Best extinguisher for fires near electronics. Good for fixed fire-fighting systems. Can break down into toxic gases when heated to high temperatures. Can dissipate quickly in ventilated areas. Because it depletes the ozone layer, halon is no longer being manufactured.
Halon substitutes (Haltron, Xintex, FE 241)	Interferes with chemical reaction. Removes enough heat to bring the material below the ignition point.	Works more quickly than CO_2 and reduces number of fire reflashes. Good for fixed fire-fighting systems and electronics. Produces gases more toxic than those produced by halon. Be sure it is approved for marine use. Can dissipate quickly in ventilated areas.

CHOOSING AN EXTINGUISHING AGENT

The key to successful fire fighting is to choose the extinguishing agent that will put out the fire with as little damage as possible. Every fire-extinguishing agent, whether in a portable or a fixed system, puts out fires by eliminating fuel, heat, or oxygen, or by breaking the chemical reaction between these components. Unfortunately, there are disadvantages to every type of extinguishing agent.

Which Extinguishing Agent Works Best

Fire Type	Extingushing Agents
A	Water works well. Multipurpose dry chemical or ABC-rated extinguishers are also appropriate. Foam is excellent and penetrates better than water. Halon and carbon dioxide (CO_2) will work, but not as effectively.
B	Carbon dioxide (CO_2), foam, dry chemical, halon, or halon substitutes are best. Water can be used as a fog or high volume spray on diesel fuel (it might spread the fire at first). Water should not be used on gasoline fires.
C	Carbon dioxide (CO_2), halon, or halon substitutes work best. The extinguishing agent must be non-conducting.
D	Use special powders or get the fire off the boat!

Using Portable Extinguishers

◆ The sequence for using portable extinguishers is:

1. **Pull** the pin.

2. **Aim** low.

3. **Squeeze** the trigger.

4. **Sweep** the base.

◆ The pin on portable fire extinguishers must be **pulled** out before the extinguishers will work.

◆ **Aim** the extinguisher at the base of the flame.

First, pull the pin on the extingusher, then aim low, squeeze the trigger, and sweep the base of the fire.

◆ Keep your face away from the top of the extinguisher, and release the contents by **squeezing** the two handles together or by opening the valve. On a cartridge-operated, dry chemical extinguisher, the puncturing lever also must be hit with the palm of the hand. Do not hold directly onto the nozzle of a CO_2 extinguisher. It gets cold enough to cause frostbite.

◆ As the extinguisher is discharging, **sweep** the base of the flame rapidly. Work quickly and aim accurately—**most extinguishers on small vessels empty themselves in 8 to 10 seconds.**

◆ Although you must be fairly close to the fire to successfully fight it with portable extinguishers, do not approach it too quickly. Be familiar with the range of your extinguishers so you don't have to go closer than necessary.

◆ Use your extinguishing agent wisely—it may last only 8 to 10 seconds.

PORTABLE EXTINGUISHERS

Portable fire extinguishers are classified and clearly marked by both a letter and number (except for class D fires, which have no number). The letters—A, B, C, or D—identify the class of fire the extinguisher will put out if it is used properly and the fire is not too large for the extinguisher. Some extinguishers work on more than one class of fire and will specify that on their label. For example, an extinguisher might be labeled BC and would be effective on class B, class C, or class BC fires.

The number on the extinguisher indicates its size. The Coast Guard uses the Roman numerals I, II, III, IV, and V to indicate the extinguisher size. The National Fire Protection Association uses Arabic numerals (2, 4, 5, etc.) to indicate the amount of fire the extinguisher will put out. In both cases, larger numbers indicate larger and heavier extinguishers. The two rating systems cannot be interchanged.

Tips for Fire Classes

◆ **Class A fires** will re-ignite if they are not totally cooled or covered with the extinguishing agent. Be very cautious working around burning fiberglass laminates, epoxies, and urethane insulating foam as they give off extremely toxic vapors.

◆ **Class B fires** must be smothered or blanketed with the proper extinguishing agent. Be extra careful not to scatter the fuel while fighting these fires or you may increase its size.

◆ **Shut the electricity off before attempting to extinguish class C fires.**

◆ Dry powders are the only type of extinguishing agent that is effective on **class D fires.** These extinguishers are very rare on recreational vessels, so make sure your emergency flares are not located near flammable sources. Do you need to move yours?

Use the Right Extinguisher

In order to put out a fire, you should use an extinguisher classified for that fire. Match extinguishers for fires that are most likely to occur in a particular area. For example, extinguishers near or in engine rooms should be rated at least BC, as a fire in this location is likely to involve flammable liquids or gases (class B) and electrical equipment (class C).

Coast Guard–approved fire extinguishers are required on certain recreational vessels. See the *Federal Requirements and Safety Tips for Recreational Boats* or call (800) 368-5647 for details.

FIXED FIRE-EXTINGUISHING SYSTEMS

A fixed system (sometimes called an automatic system) using CO_2, halon, or halon replacements can detect and extinguish small fires before they become too large to fight. It is an excellent choice for larger recreational vessels that have unmanned, enclosed spaces like engine rooms. For safety reasons, a manual activation device should be located outside the compartment containing the fixed system since everyone must be evacuated from the area before the system is discharged.

Putting out fires means that the correct extinguishing agent needs to be properly directed. That's why trained people are a vital component of successful fire fighting. **Practice** using portable extinguishers and **know** fire-fighting basics. Even if you have an automatic system, you may still need to close vents and fuel lines, and shut down engines for the system to work properly. Away from port there is no fire department to call, and the Coast Guard is mandated to put out fires on vessels only when lives are in jeopardy.

FIRE-FIGHTING TIPS

◆ Breathing smoke and gases can kill you. Watch out and stay low!

◆ **Always** keep your escape route open and clear. To maintain an uninterrupted flow of agent to the fire, have backup extinguishers and other people immediately available.

◆ **Never** turn your back on a fire. If you need to retreat, back away and keep your eyes on it.

◆ Halon, halon replacements, and CO_2 tend to blow away in windy conditions, so keep the wind at your back. This may mean turning your vessel.

◆ Fire fighting is dangerous business. Fires and decomposing halon-type agents produce **poisonous gases**. Because the vapors are invisible, you cannot determine their level of concentration by the amount of smoke in the air. When halon decomposes, it produces a sharp, acrid smell, which should be a signal to leave the area immediately. When using these extinguishing agents or fighting a fire in an enclosed area, you must either exit the area quickly or wear self-contained breathing apparatus. (Most recreational vessels won't have this apparatus, but mentioning its importance should make the point about how dangerous fire fighting can be.)

FIRE-FIGHTING STEPS

Now that you are familiar with fire, fire extinguishers, and some basic fire-fighting tips, it's time to put it all together into a strategy. When a fire is detected on board, follow these five steps. **Note: Some of these steps may occur simultaneously.**

1. Quickly Size Up the Emergency, and Notify the Coast Guard or Other Vessels.

◆ When a fire is detected, sound the alarm and get information on its type, location, and size.

◆ Notify the Coast Guard and other vessels immediately of your problem and location, since fires on small vessels can quickly involve your communications equipment.

Breaking the Fire Triangle and Stopping the Chain Reaction

1. Shut off engines, and **fuel** and gas lines that are feeding the fire.

2. Deprive the fire of **oxygen** by closing doors and hatches, and closing off ventilation systems.

3. Use the proper fire extinguisher for the class of fire.

4. To slow the fire's spread, **cool** combustible materials before they ignite. This is especially important in metal boats—which conduct heat well.

◆ How you fight the fire will depend on your vessel's arrangement, the location of the fire, and available equipment. Every vessel should have a plan for fighting fires in all spaces.

2. Rescue trapped people.

◆ Check to make sure a person really is trapped before a rescue is attempted.

◆ Stay low to avoid as much smoke and heat as possible, and **always** have a backup buddy.

◆ You may need to extinguish the fire as you do the rescue.

Courtesy of U.S. Coast Guard

3. Confine the fire to its present size and location.

◆ This is the time to shut doors and hatches, shut down engines, close off ventilation and exhaust systems, and turn off electricity and fuel lines in the fire area.

◆ Remember to check the fire's boundaries **on all sides, bottom, and top.**

4. Extinguish the fire with the least damage to people and property.

◆ Try to accomplish steps three and four simultaneously. This will cause the least damage to the vessel, its contents, and passengers. What gear and equipment is being affected by the fire?

◆ Make preparations to abandon ship while fire-fighting operations are taking place. Assign one person to prepare survival craft or other survival equipment.

◆ Abandon ship **only** if it is more dangerous to be on board than in the water. If a fire seems out of control, consider abandoning the vessel into a life raft or your tender, leaving the raft's or tender's painter line attached to the vessel until you are sure it should be cut.

5. Overhaul.

◆ Examine areas affected by the fire, clean up, and restore machinery and equipment.

◆ If water has been used to fight the fire, dewatering should begin immediately in order to maintain the vessel's stability.

◆ Before opening closed areas where halon, halon substitutes, or CO_2 have been released, make sure fires are sufficiently out. These extinguishing agents **do not** cool fires, so reflashes are possible.

◆ Examine the fire area for hot spots or embers that need to be cooled or extinguished.

◆ Be prepared to fight new fires during the overhaul. For several hours after the fire is extinguished a fire watch should be set up to check for reflash.

DOCKSIDE FIRE FIGHTING

Many fires occur while the vessel is docked or moored in a harbor. Fire-fighting steps at the dock are the same as at sea except for the luxury of accessing professional fire fighters and emergency medical workers while shoreside. The following steps will help maximize the effectiveness of shoreside fire fighters.

Stoves and Heaters

Precautions for **oil** heaters and cook stoves:

◆ Drying your clothes over or near the stove or heater is a great way to start a fire!

◆ The areas next to stoves and stovepipes (or exhaust pipes) are extremely dry and a setup for fire. Using heat shields can help prevent this.

Precautions for **propane** heaters and cook stoves:

◆ Carbon monoxide is a by-product of combustion from any fuel, and can lead to carbon monoxide poisoning if the stove or heater is not properly ventilated. **Be sure your ventilation is adequate.**

◆ Propane is heavier than air and it will flow into the lower parts of your vessel where it can be ignited easily by a spark, resulting in an explosion. This can be a problem particularly where bilges are not adequately ventilated, so **check for leaks in your propane tubing and fittings and keep your bilges aired out.**

◆ A representative from your marina or docking area should meet with fire-fighting officials to discuss ways to ensure boaters have the information needed to help fire fighters do the best job they can.

◆ Make sure the name and numbers you use to describe your dock space are the same as those used by the fire department.

◆ Know where the extinguisher is at your marina or docking area, and what type it is.

◆ Keep the dock and fire lanes free of equipment and other materials that may block fire-fighter access.

◆ If your vessel is docked near the end of the pier, make sure the local response vehicles carry enough hose to reach your vessel.

◆ Keep in mind that shoreside fire fighters may use large amounts of water or foam to put out a vessel fire regardless of the type of fire. Pumps should be engaged, if possible, to keep your vessel from sinking.

FIRE PREVENTION

Preventing vessel fires involves common sense, taking time for maintenance checks, and separating fuel, heat, and oxygen. Follow this check-off list for good fire prevention practices.

Fire Extinguishers

◆ Visually check all portable fire extinguishers and fixed systems once a month, being sure to turn all dry chemical extinguishers upside down and hit them with a rubber hammer to make sure the chemical agent is loose.

◆ Have your fire extinguishers and fixed systems checked by a certified person once a year.

◆ Refill used extinguishers as soon as possible.

Engine Room

◆ **Always** run engine room blowers for several minutes before starting gasoline engines.

◆ Install an automatic fire-extinguishing system in your unattended engine room. Be sure it has automatic engine and ventilation shutdown systems that operate before the extinguishing agent is discharged.

◆ Check to be sure fuel connections are tight.

◆ Install remote fuel shutdown valves outside the engine area.

◆ Insulate exhaust lines that lie near combustible material.

◆ Empty drip pans frequently.

◆ Check fuel and lubricating oil lines to be sure they are free of kinks. Replace brittle, cracked, or otherwise damaged lines, making sure they are arranged to prevent rubbing. They should be rated for their intended service with spray shields at bends and connections to prevent spraying of fuel in case of a leak.

◆ Use a ventilated, covered metal container for disposal of oily rags.

◆ Regularly inspect electrical wiring and hoses for cracking or damage, and replace them as needed with equipment approved for marine use.

◆ Install vapor globes, and steel or plastic cages around lights.

◆ Keep the oil in your bilge to an absolute minimum.

◆ Charge batteries in a well-ventilated area. (These produce hydrogen, a highly explosive gas.)

◆ Put batteries in a secure box so they don't tip over. Keep metal tools, etc. away from batteries so they don't fall on the terminals and cause an arc.

Electrical System

◆ Avoid overloading electrical outlets and motors.

◆ Replace loose, frayed, or worn electrical wires and short circuits promptly.

◆ Always use the proper size fuses and circuit breakers.

Accommodation Spaces

◆ Cover and protect light bulbs from contact with combustible materials.

◆ Position space heaters away from combustible materials.

◆ Install operational smoke detectors in each accommodation space and test them each month.

◆ Avoid storing combustibles next to flames or other heat sources.

◆ Replace combustible curtains and carpets with noncombustible.

◆ Be sure sleeping areas have an operable escape hatch overhead in case a fire blocks normal exit routes.

Galley

◆ Store combustible materials a safe distance from galley stove.

◆ Turn the stove off when it is unattended.

◆ Clean galley hoods, filters, and stacks regularly.

Smoking

◆ Prohibit smoking in bed and where combustible materials or flammable liquids or vapors are present.

◆ Properly dispose of cigarette butts and matches in ashtrays. (Cigarette butts thrown over the side can be blown back on board.)

◆ Empty ashtrays into empty metal containers.

Fueling

◆ Keep ignition sources and smokers away from fueling area.

◆ Take portable tanks and jugs off the boat to fill them.

◆ Wipe up any fuel spills immediately.

◆ Ventilate areas after refueling and before starting your engine.

◆ Be sure the fuel lines on your outboard motor don't leak or drip onto your battery cables.

◆ In extremely cold weather remove all sources of static electricity, including synthetic clothing, from fuel sources.

Combustible Materials

◆ Store paints, thinners, solvents, and other combustible or flammable liquids in a designated locker or storeroom with proper ventilation.

◆ Store cardboard boxes, plywood, and other combustible materials away from heat sources.

◆ Stow portable fuel tanks or jerry jugs securely on deck in an upright position.

◆ Store "heavier than air" gases away from accommodation spaces, and be sure the valves, pressure regulators, and pipes leading from these cylinders are protected from damage.

Training

◆ Everyone on board should know where the fire extinguishers are and how to use them.

◆ Hold regular fire drills, or at least talk about drill procedures.

Good fire prevention practices will eliminate the need to test your fire-fighting skills.

Safe Seamanship

Chapter
13

Courtesy of U.S. Coast Guard

The dazed crew of a Japanese trawler was plucked out of the Sea of Japan earlier this year clinging to the wreckage of their sunken ship. They claimed that a cow, falling out of a clear blue sky, had struck the trawler amidships, shattering its hull and sinking the vessel within minutes.

The Russian Air Force reluctantly informed Japanese authorities that the crew of one of its cargo planes had apparently stolen a cow wandering at the edge of a Siberian airfield. According to the report, they rustled the cow into the plane's hold and took off for home. Unprepared for live cargo, the Russian crew was ill-equipped to manage a frightened cow rampaging within the hold. To save the aircraft and themselves, they shoved the bovine out of the cargo hatch as they crossed the Sea of Japan at an altitude of 30,000 feet.

Alaska Fisherman's Journal, June 1997

Hopefully, your problems afloat will not be as extreme as falling cows. What follows are some safety concerns not addressed in other areas of this book: Anchoring, Standing Watch, Buoys, Land Structures, Navigation Lights, Radar Reflectors, Rules of the Road, Legal Concerns, Stability, Groundings, Coast Guard Emergency Pumps, Loss of Power or Steering, and Towing.

ANCHORING

Knowing how to safely anchor up is an important boating skill, and one that more than one person on board should have. The anchor itself should be readily available at all times in case it needs to be set quickly in an emergency.

Try to anchor in good holding ground like clay, mud, or firm sand. Slowly lower your anchor off the bow until it hits bottom. Then drift or power back until you have let line out that is six to eight times the depth of the bottom. For example, if you are anchoring in 30 feet of water, you should have 180' to 240' of line out. If you expect some adverse weather, let out line ten times the depth of water. Be sure your anchor is secured to a strong point on the foredeck and set up an anchor watch schedule.

These general guidelines for the length of your anchor line need to be used with wisdom. Take into account other factors such as tides and where you are anchoring. In tight bays and crowded anchorages too much line can allow you to swing into the beach or your neighbor's wheelhouse!

Anchor.

STANDING WATCH

Be sure your wheel watch understands what he's doing before standing watch. At a minimum a wheel watch should know basic rules of the road, whistle and radio distress signals, standard running lights, how to use the boat's electronics, and when to call the captain. If you have a magnetic compass, everyone standing watch should know how to use it and the compass deviation table. If you have enough people on board, try to pair a greenhorn with an experienced hand on the same watch, and give orders to get someone to take over if they become sleepy.

Be sure you understand the effect of currents on your boat. If you don't know what the currents are for your area, look them up in a Current Table. When the weather or current makes passage of a particular stretch of water so difficult you only **think** you can make it, remember that the good seaman admits his own limitations and those of his boat, and only does what he **knows** he can do safely.

Keep a dead-reckoning plot on a chart whenever underway in fog, even if you have every available piece of modern, red-hot electronic gear. Also, consider keeping a logbook with entries every 15-30 minutes, or during course changes, showing time, location, speed, direction, etc. This will give you excellent backup in case of electronic failure.

Fast and Slow-Moving Hazards

Personal watercraft (Jet-Skis™) can be a hazard due to their sudden and unexpected movements. Kayaks, canoes, and other slow-moving vessels are also a possible problem for skippers because they can be difficult to spot and cannot quickly change course. Keep a sharp lookout for both fast and slow-moving hazards!

D. Brenner

When recreational boaters are near large commercial ships, the responsibility for getting out of the way is on the person standing watch on the recreational boat. You should assume that the commercial ship can't see you, can't maneuver out of harm's way, and can't stop in time.

Large commercial ships need a lot of space to stop and turn. Even a medium-size cargo vessel may need $2\frac{1}{2}$ miles to stop in an emergency. Commercial craft are operating with a small crew because of automation, so lookouts may be minimal. Due to requirements for automated radios, in the future commercial ships may not be required to stand by the usual radio frequencies such as channel 16 VHF. So **drive defensively** when you are in busy commercial traffic areas on the water.

BUOYS

All of coastal North and South America use the same buoyage system to mark areas safe for navigation with standard shapes, colors, numbering, and position.

Although buoys can be invaluable aids to navigation, their lights may burn out, they can shift location or capsize, or they may be carried away by the tide, ice, or a vessel. If buoys don't appear to be where the chart says they should be, they may not be there. Beware!

Standard American Buoys

Returning from sea[1]	Color	Number	Unlighted buoy shapes[2]	Light color[3]	Daymark shapes[4]
Right side of channel	Red	Even	Nun	Red	Triangular
Left side of channel	Green	Odd	Can	Green	Square
Mid-channel	Red & white vertical stripes	May be lettered	Nun or Can	White	Octagonal

[1] Or heading in a northerly direction along the Pacific Coast, south and west along the Atlantic and Gulf coasts, clockwise around a significant land mass, or in the general direction of a flood tide.

[2] If the buoy is unlighted, it will have this shape. The small figure next to the buoy will be this color.

[3] If the buoy has a light, instead of a specific shape, the light on the buoy will be this color.

[4] A daymark, a small marker held up by poles and visible only during daylight hours, may also be present.

Small symbols on the right appear on charts.

LAND STRUCTURES

Power Lines

Overhead power lines can be bad news for boaters, so be sure you have enough clearance and then some when launching and underway, especially for your vessel's masts and antennas. Don't count on lightning-strike protection; it won't help you if you contact a power line.

During a flood, it can be exciting to explore newly created waterways in small boats, but floods can also cause power lines to go down, creating huge electrical charges in the water.

Bridges

Boats are supposed to **pass under** bridges, not hit them. If you want to be sure you don't end up in the newspaper or on the nightly news, find out what the clearances are for the bridges in your boating area, as well as the tides or seasonal variations in the water level of rivers and lakes. Water depth under bridges is often marked, and bridge heights are usually published in nautical charts. If you boat where there are drawbridges, be sure to inquire about the rules and protocols ahead of time.

Boating traffic, current, tide, and water flow caused by storms can all affect your ability to navigate under bridges. Be sure to give larger vessels priority because they often have less maneuverability than you do.

Dams

Recreational boaters on lakes that have been formed by dammed rivers should be aware that the areas **above and below** these dams are extremely hazardous. Many areas are well identified with suitable warnings. Although the hazards are obvious at the top, they may not be quite so apparent at the dam's downriver side, especially on dams of shorter heights.

An unexpected flow of water from a dam can create sudden, turbulent conditions downstream. Perhaps less evident is the hydraulic backwash created by the flow of water over a dam. **Boaters who get too close to the downstream side of a dam can be sucked into the backwash current and forced under water over and over, unable to escape.** This is the type of recycling **you do not** want to experience.

NAVIGATION LIGHTS

Navigation lights tell you a great deal about what nearby boats are doing. Check out the requirements for your vessel by looking in the U.S. Coast Guard's *Federal Requirements and Safety Tips for Recreational Boats* booklet. (See Chapter 14, Resources.) The book will also help you learn to identify the vessel lights you are most likely to encounter.

RADAR REFLECTORS

Unless you're doing stealth work, you want other boats to see you, especially at night and in foggy conditions. If your boat is non-metallic you are not going to be very visible on another ship's radar, and collisions will be more likely unless you have a radar reflector. This inexpensive metal device makes it easier for others to detect your boat on radar, especially if it is placed as high as possible on the vessel and clear of obstructions.

RULES OF THE ROAD

All vessels are governed by the Navigation Rules: International-Inland. (See Chapter 14, Resources.) You can help keep your vessel off a collision course by knowing these rules and remembering that it may be necessary to deviate from the rules in order to avoid immediate danger.

Lookout

It is illegal for all hands to sleep while a vessel is underway or drifting. You must maintain a proper lookout at all times by sight and hearing, as well as by all available means appropriate (including radar). This constant watch allows you to fully appraise the situation and the risk of collision.

Safe Speed

You must proceed at a safe speed at all times so you can take action to avoid collisions, and can stop within a distance appropriate for the prevailing circumstances and conditions. Safe speed also means respecting other users of the water, including marine mammals.

Priorities

To help vessel operators make decisions on traffic flow, some vessels have priority over others. **You must give way to vessels above you on this list.**

1. Vessel not under command

2. Vessel restricted in its ability to maneuver

3. Vessel constrained by its draft

4. Vessel engaged in commercial fishing

5. Sailing vessel

6. Overtaken vessel

7. Power-driven vessel

8. Seaplane

Note: In a narrow channel, vessels restricted to the channel have priority over fishing vessels, sailing vessels, and vessels under 20 meters.

Avoid Collision

When a collision at sea occurs between two vessels, both operators usually share the blame in the incident. Thus the familiar boating term "right of way" is a bit inaccurate since boaters who insist on their "right" and thus get involved in a collision will be found at least partially to blame.

The Zones of Approach define your action and relationship to another vessel. Based on the priorities noted above and your specific circumstance, you will know when you need to **give way** to another vessel. The vessel that gives way should take early and substantial action to keep well clear.

In general, the vessel passing another vessel is the **give-way vessel**. The vessel being passed is the **stand on vessel**, and should keep its speed and course constant until passed.

When meeting **head-on,** vessels should pass port-to-port unless they have clearly communicated other intentions to one another over the radio.

In a **crossing** situation, **if your vessel is approaching another vessel's port forward side, you are the give-way vessel.** Keep out of the way and, as far as possible, avoid crossing ahead of the vessel. When in doubt whether a situation is crossing or head-on, assume it's head-on and act accordingly.

If your vessel has priority, it is your duty to see that a collision is avoided. As such, maintain course and speed, but be prepared to act if the give-way vessel does not take appropriate action. Risk of a collision exists if another vessel's compass bearing doesn't change or changes very little relative to you. When in doubt, chicken out; assume the risk of collision exists and take action.

You can help avoid collisions by not passing ahead of another vessel, by taking early and positive action, by making obvious course and speed changes, and by slowing, stopping, or reversing if necessary.

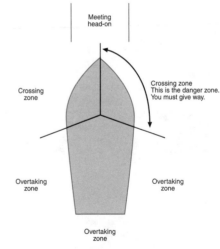

Zones of approach.

Slow Down!

Is the weather rough?	**Slow down!**
Are the seas rough?	**Slow down!**
Is your vessel unstable?	**Slow down!**
Are you turning too fast?	**Slow down!**
Is the visibility poor?	**Slow down!**
Are the waters crowded?	**Slow down!**

D. Brenner

Sound Signals

You must have some sound making device on board. See the *Navigation Rules: International-Inland* and your state laws for specific requirements for your vessel. When there is danger or doubt as to who is doing what, the signal is **five or more short blasts.**

It is sometimes very difficult to hear another vessel's horn. In these cases, radio communication with the other vessel may be necessary to determine the intention. It helps to monitor the emergency frequencies on your radios. (See page 51.)

STABILITY

Jefferson City, Missouri—Ten people were in a 14-foot boat with a 20-hp engine going up the Missouri River when it swamped. All 10 were thrown into the water. The nine people who were wearing PFDs survived. The person who drowned had a PFD in the boat, but he wasn't wearing it.

Ten people in a 14-foot boat!? Wow! Overloading can create serious stability problems with disastrous results.

The term stability refers to the ability of a vessel to return to the upright position after being heeled by an external force, and can be viewed as the relationship between a vessel's buoyancy and its load. The load can be people, gear, supplies, or unplanned weight such as water on deck.

Stability problems often result from a combination of factors and frequently involve a change in weather or sea conditions. Factors that change a vessel's buoyancy or load, or cause the load to shift, can lead to a change in stability that could be life-threatening.

You can reduce your chances of capsizing by taking steps to ensure that your vessel remains stable enough for your operating conditions.

Built-in Flotation

All commercially made recreational vessels under 20 feet are required to have enough built-in flotation to float the vessel if it turns over. This flotation is often built into the seats, and **it should not be removed!**

Environmental Factors

◆ The first rule in rough weather seamanship is to **slow down!** This gives your vessel more time to adjust to the seas, keeps more water off your decks, gives you a more comfortable ride, and increases the time you have to react.

◆ Certain sea conditions and other environmental factors can reduce your vessel's stability. Beam seas can be dangerous because they pour large amounts of shifting water on deck, and can create problems if the water isn't quickly drained.

Legal Concerns

Accident Reporting Requirements are listed on page 116.

Negligent Operation
Penalties can be imposed for negligent operation. Some examples of negligent operation are operating a vessel in a swimming area; operating under the influence of drugs and alcohol; excessive speed; hazardous water skiing; bow riding; and riding on seat backs, transoms, or gunwales.

Rendering Assistance
The master or person in charge of the vessel is obligated by law to provide safe assistance to any individual in danger at sea. Violators are subject to a fine or imprisonment for failure to do so.

Termination of Use
A Coast Guard boarding officer may direct the operator of a vessel to correct a hazardous condition including ordering it to return to harbor. Reasons a voyage may be terminated include insufficient number of PFDs or fire extinguishers; overloading; improper lights, ventilation, or backflame protection; fuel in bilge or fuel leakage; and manifestly unsafe voyage.

◆ Large following seas are especially problematic and should be avoided because of the resultant corkscrew-type rolling, the tendency to lose the ability to steer the vessel when the rudder and propeller are out of the water, and the propensity for the vessel to broach. Icing can also create serious stability problems.

Watertight Integrity

◆ Much of a vessel's stability rests on its ability to be buoyant, which demands that dry spaces stay dry, so keep your vessel's flush hatches secure at all times. In addition, regularly check and clean the hatch's seating surface and gasket to make sure it will seat properly.

◆ In rough weather, keep doors and hatches closed and secured to prevent water from entering the wrong places. A dutch door to the galley can permit good ventilation but keep water out when the weather is tough.

◆ Install bilge alarms and check the bilge on a regular basis. Bilge alarms are cheap insurance.

Load Size and Freeboard

◆ Make sure your boat's load is balanced from front to back, and side to side.

◆ Tie your cargo down so it cannot shift.

◆ Never exceed the loading capacity of your vessel. Commercially made single-hull vessels less than 20 feet (except sailboats, canoes, kayaks, and inflatables) are rated for the total weight, number of people, and size engine they can safely carry. This information is stated on a U.S. Coast Guard Maximum Capacities Label installed on the vessel. **If the weather is rough, carry fewer.** Following these recommendations can help save your life.

U.S. COAST GUARD

MAXIMUM CAPACITIES

XX PERSONS OR XXX LBS

YELLOW

XX LBS, PERSONS, MOTORS, GEAR
XXX HP MOTOR

If your vessel does not have a capacity label, the following formula can serve as a guideline for the capacity of your vessel:

$$\text{Number of People} = \frac{\text{Length of Boat x Width of Boat (in feet)}}{15}$$

◆ Overloaded vessels are often dangerously unstable and compromised in several ways. Because extra cargo is usually carried on deck, the vessel's center of gravity is raised. This slows the vessel's roll, and generally decreases the tendency of the boat to return to its normal upright position. In addition, the extra weight sets the vessel deeper in the water, causing a decrease in the amount of freeboard. This is not a good situation.

◆ Freeboard is critical because it represents the reserve buoyancy in a hull. With low or no freeboard, the ability of a ship to return to the upright position becomes severely compromised. Low freeboard also means more waves coming on board. This means additional weight on deck, free surface effect problems, and even less freeboard than before. See Chapter 14, Resources for further information about stability.

GROUNDINGS

It is difficult for a vessel to occupy a space in the water already filled by a rock or sand. Although some rocks may not be charted properly, the vast majority of those that have been struck are charted. Most boat groundings happen because somebody "goofed."

Avoidance is the best defense against grounding, and for that you need good charts and full attention to navigation. Try out difficult passages for the first time in daylight and with a rising tide, go slowly, and post a lookout on the bow.

If you do end up aground, call for assistance and do not attempt to refloat until you have inspected the damage as best you can. If your vessel has a deep hull, you may need to use your anchors to the side and/or boards propped up under the rail to keep your boat from heeling over too far. Be sure to make the vessel as watertight as possible before you try to refloat it on a rising tide. If you are taking on water, call for assistance again. You may need to beach your vessel until either you can repair the damage or assistance arrives.

Holed Vessel

When flooding occurs you want to plug, close, and pump!

◆ **Plug** any holes if you can do it quickly. Small holes can be plugged with almost any material on hand, including a wooden plug wrapped in cloth, so keep several aboard your vessel.

◆ **Close** all through-hull fittings (you do know where they are, don't you?), and any adjacent areas to slow the flooding.

◆ **Pump!** Use vessel pumps and bail by hand. An excited skipper might be able to save his boat with a 5-gallon bucket.

◆ Larger holes may take more time to plug. One good method is to place a pillow over the hole, hold it tightly, and brace it by any handy means. A collision mat, mattress, or tarp secured at each outside corner can be dragged under the vessel to cover the hole, too. The water pressure and tightly secured lines will hold it against the hull and reduce water flow. Get to a safe harbor or beach fast and prepare to abandon the vessel if necessary.

◆ If your vessel is holed near the waterline and is set up so you can cause a deliberate list—perhaps by swinging out a heavy object on the end of a boom, or transferring fuel or gear from one side to another—consider doing this on the side opposite the hole to reduce the pressure at the damaged spot. **Do not** do this if the list will make your vessel dangerously unstable.

◆ If you cannot control the flooding, call for assistance.

168

COAST GUARD EMERGENCY PUMPS

◆ If you neglected to carry emergency high water pumps, or your pumps cannot keep up with incoming water, the Coast Guard can provide you with emergency, gasoline-powered pumps. Note: These pumps cannot be delivered instantly, so call for help early!

◆ The type you are most likely to get comes sealed in a rectangular orange plastic container about 3 feet high, and is capable of pumping about 120 gallons per minute. Release the clips and lift the top off to open it, but don't smoke—there will be gasoline fumes inside. Keep the canister upright when you remove the pump or the oil may drain from the pump's crankcase, and the engine might seize on starting. There will be a waterproof flashlight and instructions in the canister.

◆ Follow the instructions or the pump will not work. Do not cut off the end of the discharge hose (this will prevent the pump from priming itself). Do make sure the O-ring is inside and flat in the threaded end of the intake hose. Finally, don't over-choke it or it may not start.

USCG Drop Pump Instructions

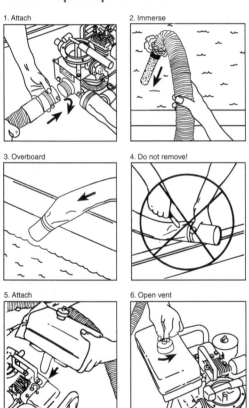

1. Attach
2. Immerse
3. Overboard
4. Do not remove!
5. Attach
6. Open vent

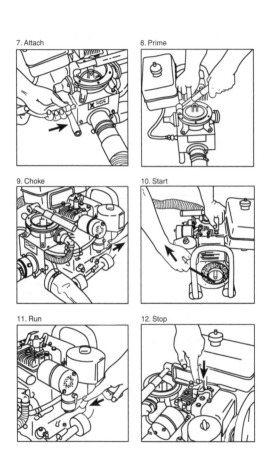

7. Attach
8. Prime
9. Choke
10. Start
11. Run
12. Stop

Useful Facts and Figures

- 1 knot = 1.15 mph
- fathom = 6 feet
- 120 fathoms = 1 cable
- 7.5 cables = 1 statute mile
- 8.44 cables = 1 nautical mile
- 6,076 feet (about 2,000 yards) = 1 nautical mile = 1 minute of latitude
- 32 points of the compass = 360 degrees
- 1 point of the compass = 11.25 degrees
- 1 gallon of freshwater = 8.355 pounds
- 1 cubic foot = 7.481 gallons of water
- 1 cubic foot of freshwater = 62.5 pounds
- 1 cubic foot of salt water = 64 pounds
- 1 ton of freshwater = 35.84 cubic feet
- 1 ton of salt water = 35 cubic feet
- 261.8 gallons of seawater = 1 ton
- 1 cubic foot of normal storage ice = 62 pounds
- 1 barrel (42 gallons) of diesel fuel = 315 pounds
- 1 gallon of engine motor oil = about 7.3 pounds
- Doubling the diameter of a pipe increases the carrying capacity of the pipe four times.

LOSS OF POWER OR STEERING

◆ Occasionally vessels lose their propeller or steering, or suffer engine breakdown. When this occurs, the vessel is suddenly plunged into a totally helpless situation and immediate assistance should be requested. The Coast Guard much prefers to be told "No further assistance required" when halfway there, than to lose the head start on a case.

◆ If you lose power or steering, anchor if you can. Often, however, the water will be too deep. If you are in open water far from land, and you don't have a commercially made sea anchor, make one. Anything that drags under water is a sea anchor—even a bucket or your regular anchor. When streamed over the bow on at least 60 feet of line, a good sea anchor reduces the drift due to wind, and the boat will ride better, holding its head out of the trough.

Sea anchor

◆ Weather permitting, you may be able to tow the boat, or at least somewhat control the direction of drift, if you have a skiff.

TOWING

Many mariners will eventually need a tow. At best, towing can be an inconvenience or perhaps a bit of an embarrassment. At worst, it can and has led to tragedy because there is more to towing than just throwing a line and going. It is hazardous work often left to the professionals. If you decide to tow, follow these steps:

Making the Decision

◆ The decision to tow or abandon the vessel must be made carefully. It is difficult for many vessel owners and operators to decide to abandon their vessel even if that is the only safe alternative, but the primary consideration to be made in this case is safety.

◆ Before you can safely tow the boat in question you need the right size tow lines. A line breaking under load can snap back and seriously injure or crush people. A tow line of sufficient strength and length should be part of every boater's basic equipment inventory.

◆ Braided nylon line is superior to three-strand nylon for towing because it is stronger, has more elasticity, and is more resistant to chafing.

◆ Before deciding to tow a vessel, consider the following:

• Can the problem be fixed with a part being brought out?

• Is the weather improving or deteriorating?

• If the vessel being towed capsizes, will it endanger the crew and towing vessel?

• Is the disabled vessel taking on water? If so, **do not attempt to tow it until the flooding is controlled!**

◆ The bottom line is, no vessel is worth a human life!

◆ If you choose not to tow the vessel, stand by until assistance arrives.

◆ Contact the Coast Guard to tell them about the situation.

Towing Preparation

Before approaching the disabled vessel, get your equipment ready.

◆ Have a sharp knife or axe nearby to cut the tow line if needed.

◆ Make sure all involved know their duties ahead of time.

◆ Everyone on deck on both vessels should wear their PFDs.

◆ Double all watches and be prepared for the unexpected.

◆ The vessel to be towed should have all gear stowed and its anchor ready in case the tow line breaks. To help the towed vessel track better, its weight should be distributed slightly so the vessel squats in the stern.

Approaching the Disabled Vessel

◆ Make a complete circle of the vessel to inspect it as closely as possible.

◆ Decide on your approach based on sea state, wind, tide, current, size of the vessels, nearby hazards, maneuvering characteristics of your boat, method of passing the tow line, and the drift rate of the disabled vessel.

◆ When passing the tow line to the vessel in distress, do not use your hands or legs to keep the vessels apart. It is much preferable to damage a boat hook than a body!

Connecting the Tow Line

Tows often involve the use of a single-point tow line—a V or a Y bridle.

◆ Single-point tow lines can be used when there is a towing bitt or other attachment point along the centerline of the towing vessel forward of the rudder.

Single point

◆ V bridles can be rigged with the open end of the V on either the stern of the towing vessel or the bow of the distressed vessel.

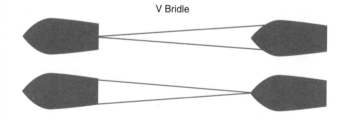

V Bridle

◆ Y bridles require two lengths of tow line.

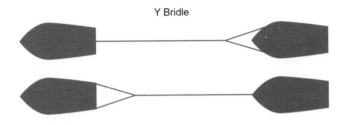

Y Bridle

◆ Only the people essential for the tow should remain on board the towed vessel to help steer it.

Getting Started

◆ The key word during a tow is **slow.** Take up the strain slowly when starting the tow, and follow the manufacturer's towing hull speed recommendations. Even six knots is too fast for most displacement hulls.

◆ Stability of the disabled vessel is of primary concern.

◆ Designate a person on the towing vessel to monitor the towed vessel and keep the towing vessel's propellers from being fouled by the tow line. The tow watch should be wearing a PFD, plus have a backup person, and be ready to quickly cut the tow line if necessary.

Underway

◆ Contact the Coast Guard to set up a communications schedule.

◆ Adjust the tow line so that both vessels will be on top of waves at the same time. This will result in a smoother tow and less strain.

◆ Seas put a considerable strain on the vessels, tow line, and deck fittings. In heavy seas, shock loading can be diminished by increasing the scope (length) of the tow line, reducing speed, and quartering the seas. Reducing speed is more effective than increasing the length of the tow line.

Securing the Tow

◆ Slow down **before** arriving at your destination. Inside a harbor you may need to bring the towed vessel alongside to maneuver safely.

◆ Prepare fenders, and keep hands from between vessels and the dock.

◆ Inform the Coast Guard of your arrival.

◆ Recover, restore, and stow all towing gear.

Putting It All Together

There's a lot more to boating than just untying lines and pointing your boat. With lives, vessels, and livelihoods at stake, it pays to take the extra time to be prepared and to know what you're doing. Besides, you don't want to go out there and look like a complete yahoo, do you?

Resources

Courtesy of AMSEA

This chapter lists suggested books, recommended videos, and agencies to contact for first aid, CPR, and marine safety training and information.

RECOMMENDED REFERENCES

The following references would be helpful to have on board. Many change periodically so check to be sure yours are up to date.

- *Chapman Piloting: Seamanship and Small Boat Handling*, E.S. Maloney, ed., Hearst Marine Books, New York, 1994, 62nd edn., 656 pp.

- Charts, in sufficient scale and detail for safe navigation.

- *Coast Pilot,* U.S. Government Printing Office. Get the one appropriate to your region. Available from U.S. Government Printing Office, (888) 293-6498, gpoaccess@gpo.gov.

- *Emergencies at Sea,* by Sid Stapleton, Hearst Marine Books, New York, 1991, 223 pp.

- *Federal Requirements and Safety Tips for Recreational Boats.* Available through the U.S. Coast Guard Infoline, (800) 368-5647 or from your local U.S. Coast Guard resource.

- *Light List,* Coast Guard Publication COMDTPUB #P16502.6. Available from U.S. Government Printing Office, (888) 293-6498, gpoaccess@gpo.gov.

- *Local Notice to Mariners.* Available through your regional Coast Guard office.

- *Navigation Rules: International-Inland.* Available from U.S. Government Printing Office, (888) 293-6498, gpoaccess@gpo.gov.

- Tidal Current Tables

- Tide Tables

- *Water Wise: Safety for the Recreational Boater,* by J. Dzugan and S. Jensen, University of Alaska Sea Grant MAB-51, Fairbanks, 1999 (this volume).

BOOKS ON MARINE SAFETY AND SURVIVAL

Adrift, by S. Callahan. Houghton-Mifflin, 1986, 344 pp. Six days after he set sail from the Canary Islands for the Caribbean, Callahan's 21-foot sloop *Solo Napoleon* sank, and he abandoned ship into a life raft with three pounds of food and eight pints of water. Callahan's tale about his 76 days adrift over 1,800 miles before being rescued near Guadaloupe made the *New York Times* best-seller list.

Desperate Journeys, Abandoned Souls, by E. Leslie, Houghton Mifflin, Boston, 1988, 586 pp. An excellent collection of stories about survivors from historical times to the present; provides many insights into the psychological aspects of survival.

Discovering Wild Plants: Alaska, Western Canada and the Northwest, by J.J. Schofield, Alaska Northwest Books, Anchorage, 1989, 354 pp. Excellent reference full of color plates and interesting text, with a recipe on almost every page.

Edible? Incredible!, by V. Pill and M. Furlong, Pill Enterprises, Shelton, WA, 1985, 73 pp. Good information on identifying and cooking edible seafood, although it ignores paralytic shellfish poisoning problems.

Endurance: Shackleton's Incredible Voyage, by A. Lansing, McGraw Hill, New York, 1959, 282 pp. This story of Ernest Shackleton's ill-fated expedition to reach the South Pole in 1914 is particularly insightful in terms of the vital role a leader can play in a survival situation. One of the all-time great survival stories.

Field Guide to Edible Wild Plants, by B. Augier, Stackpole Books, 1974, 256 pp.

Gulf Coast Fishing Vessel Crewman's Handbook, by D. Hollin, 1989, 32 pp. Sea Grant College Program, Texas A&M University, (409) 845-3857. Geared for commercial fishermen, but full of useful information.

Keep Clear: Big Ships in Chesapeake Bay. Brochure. Maryland Sea Grant Program, University of Maryland, (301) 405-6376.

Lightning and Sailboats, by E.M. Thompson, 1992, 24 pp. Florida Sea Grant College Program, (352) 392-1837.

Marine Fire Prevention, Fire Fighting and Fire Safety, Maritime Training Advisory Board, Maritime Administration, U.S. Department of Transportation. Available from U.S. Government Printing Office, (888) 293-6498, gpoaccess@gpo.gov.

National Transportation Safety Board (NTSB) Reports. The NTSB has authority to investigate aircraft, train, bus, and fishing vessel accidents. It usually limits marine investigations to accidents involving ships of at least 100 gross tons valued at more than $500,000, or when six or more lives are lost. It also holds hearings when accidents of a potentially recurring nature happen, or if there is widespread public interest. Their reports have recommendations to prevent similar accidents. Available from National Technical Information Service, 5285 Port Royal Road, Springfield, VA 22161, (800) 553-6847, http://www.ntis.gov/search.htm.

Our Last Chance, by B. Butler and S. Butler, Exmart Press, Miami, FL, 1991, 313 pp. The Butlers set off to circumnavigate the world in their 38-foot sailboat *Siboney,* but ended up adrift in a life raft 1,200 miles west of Panama. They were rescued after 66 days by the Costa Rica Coast Guard who was looking for a lost fishing boat.

Safety at Sea: A Guide for Fishing Vessel Owners and Operators, D. Hollin, compiler, 1982, 38 pp. Sea Grant College Program, Texas A&M University, (409) 845-3857.

Safety Standards for Backyard Boat Builders, U.S. Coast Guard publication COMDTPUD P167613. Good information on safety and stability for folks who are building their own boats. Available from U.S. Government Printing Office, (888) 293-6498, gpoaccess@gpo.gov.

Shackleton's Boat Journey, by F.A. Worsley, W.W. Norton, New York, 1977, 220 pp. This book describes the same Shackleton expedition as Lansing's *Endurance,* from the ship captain's perspective.

Survive the Savage Sea, by D. Robertson, Sheridan House, Dobbs Ferry, NY, 1992, 217 pp. This account details the Robertsons' survival after their 43-foot schooner *Lucette* was attacked by killer whales and sank in 60 seconds west of the Galapagos Islands. Adrift with a life raft and dinghy were the Robertson family of five and a 22-year-old man who had joined them in Panama. They were rescued by a Japanese fishing vessel after 37 days adrift.

Survivor, by M. Greenwald (S. Callahan and D. Robertson, eds.), Blue Horizon Press, San Diego, CA, 1989, 600 pp. This is one of the more comprehensive books ever done on sea survival and is full of true stories. No major topic relating to sea survival has been left out.

Vessel Safety Manual, North Pacific Fishing Vessel Owners Association (NPFVOA), 1900 W. Emerson #101, Fishermen's Terminal, Seattle, WA 98119. Geared for commercial fishermen, but full of good marine safety information.

What Responsible Boaters Can Do to Keep Florida's Waters Clean, 1998, 10 pp. Florida Sea Grant College Program, (352) 392-1837.

117 Days Adrift, by M. Bailey and M. Bailey, Sheridan House, Dobbs Ferry, NY, 1992, 192 pp. After their yacht *Auralyn* was holed by a wounded whale 250 miles northeast of the Galapagos Islands, the Baileys abandoned ship into their life raft and dinghy. They drifted for nearly four months before being rescued by a Korean fishing boat. Their incredible tale is well documented in the extensive logs they kept.

CD-ROM

Dangerous Waters! Recreational Boating Safety Game, 1999. An interactive CD-ROM boating safety game for individual users and public exhibits. Oregon Sea Grant Program, (541) 737-2716

FIRST AID AND CPR TRAINING

For information on first aid and CPR training inquire at your local fire department, ambulance service, American Red Cross, American Heart Association, maritime academy, or captain's licensing schools. First aid training that is specifically designed for mariners or for people away from immediate assistance will be most helpful.

MARINE SAFETY AND SURVIVAL TRAINING

These organizations provide marine safety and survival training and information, or can refer you to people who do.

Alaska Marine Safety Education Association (AMSEA)
P.O. Box 2592
Sitka, AK 99835
(907) 747-3287
www.uaf.edu/seagrant/amsea/

Alaska Vocational Technical Center (AVTEC)
P.O. Box 889
Seward, AK 99664
(907) 224-3322
www.educ.state.ak.us/avtec/home.htm

American Boat and Yacht Council
3069 Solomon's Island Rd.
Edgewater, MD 21037
(410) 956-1050

BOAT/U.S. Foundation
880 S. Pickett Street
Alexandria, VA 22304
(800) 336-BOAT
In Virginia call (800) 245-BOAT
www.boatus.com

Clatsop Community College
Marine Sciences Division
1653 Jerome Avenue
Astoria, OR 97103
(503) 325-0910

Coast-Wise Marine Safety Training
Bev Noll
1385 Pebble Beach Drive
Crescent City, CA 95531
(707) 465-4400

Educational Training Company
P.O. Box 464
Sitka, AK 99835
(907) 747-5454

Fremont Maritime Services
501 N. 36th Street, #217
Seattle, WA 98103
(206) 522-5377

Mid-Atlantic Safety and Survival
P.O. Box 8453
Norfolk, VA 23503
(804) 661-3845

Marine & Industrial Safety Assoc.
P.O. Box 1978
Port Isabel, TX 78578
(956) 943-7935

McMillan Offshore Survival Training, Inc.
RR 4, Box 108
Belfast, ME 04915
(207) 338-1603

National Fire Protection Association
1 Batterymarch Park
P.O. Box 9101
Quincy, MA 02269-9101
(617) 770-3000
www.nfpa.org

National Safe Boating Council
P.O. Box 1058
Delaware, OH 43015
(614) 666-3009
www.SafeBoatingCouncil.org

NPFVOA Vessel Safety Program
(North Pacific Fishing Vessel Owners Association)
1900 West Emerson, # 101
Seattle, WA 98119
(206) 285-3383
www.halcyon.com/npfvoa

Sea Grant College Program
Texas A&M University
1716 Briarcrest, # 702
Bryan, TX 77802
(409) 845-3857
dhollin@unix.tamv.edu

Thompson Maritime, Inc.
5050 Industrial Rd.
Farmingdale, NJ 07727-3651
(732) 751-0535

U.S. Coast Guard
Office of Boating Safety
www.uscgboating.org

U.S. Coast Guard Infoline
(800) 368-5647

Resources

**U5.S. Coast Guard
Recreational Boating Safety Specialists:**

1st Coast Guard District
408 Atlantic Avenue
Boston, MA 02210
(617) 223-8464

5th Coast Guard District
Federal Building
431 Crawford Street
Portsmouth, VA 23704-5004
(757) 398-6204

7th Coast Guard District
909 SE First Avenue
Miami, FL 33131-3050
(305) 536-4497

8th Coast Guard District
Hale Boggs Federal Building
501 Magazine Street
New Orleans, LA 70130
(504) 589-6770

9th Coast Guard District
1240 E. 9th Street
Cleveland, OH 44119-2060
(216) 902-6000

11th Coast Guard District
Coast Guard Island, Bldg. 51-1
Alameda, CA 94501-5100
(510) 437-5364

13th Coast Guard District
915 Second Avenue
Seattle, WA 98174-1067
(206) 220-7257

14th Coast Guard District
300 Ala Moana Boulevard
Honolulu, HI 96850
(808) 541-2161

17th Coast Guard District
P.O. Box 25517
Juneau, AK 99802-5517
(907) 463-2297
www.uscg.mil/d17/d17rbs/d17rbs.htm

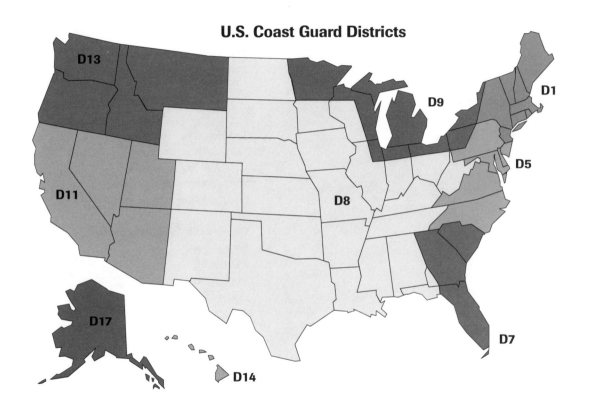

U.S. Coast Guard Districts

D13

D11

D17

D14

D9

D1

D5

D8

D7

Marine Safety & Survival Training (continued)

U.S. Coast Guard Auxiliary
(800) 336-BOAT
In Virginia call (800) 245-BOAT
www.cgaux.org

United States Marine Safety Association
1900 Arch Street
Philadelphia, PA 19103-1498
(215) 564-3484

U.S. Power Squadrons
(888) 367-8777
www.usps.org

U.S. Sailing Association
P.O. Box 1260
Portsmouth, RI 02871
(401) 683-0800
www.ussailing.org

Vessel Safety Corporation
Paul Helland
P.O. Box 2075
Kingston, RI 02881
(401) 783-5616

University of Washington Sea Grant
Sara Fisken
1735 W. Thurman Street
West Wall Building, #124
Seattle, WA 98199
(206) 543-1225

University of Washington Sea Grant
Steve Harbell
P.O. Box 88
South Bend, WA 98586
(360) 875-9331

BOATING SAFETY VIDEOTAPES

These videos can be purchased from the producers. Many are available for rent or purchase from safety training agencies, or you might find them in your local library.

Video Titles:

- *Fire Prevention and Control.* Preventing and fighting fires at sea.

- *Fishing Vessel Stability.* General points about fishing vessel stability and stability testing.

- *Medical Emergencies at Sea.* Treating medical emergencies at sea.

- *Safety Equipment and Survival Procedures.* Maydays, life raft launching, and survival kits.

Available from:

NPFVOA Vessel Safety Program
(North Pacific Fishing Vessel Owners Association)
1900 West Emerson, # 101
Seattle, WA 98119, (206) 285-3383
www.halcyon.com/npfvoa

Video Titles:

- *Emergency Radio Procedures.*

- *Inflatable Life Rafts.* Installing, launching, and boarding inflatable life rafts.

- *Personal Flotation Devices.* Types of PFDs and how they work.

- *Visual Distress Signals.* The use of pyrotechnics, radios, and lights as emergency signals.

Available from:

John Sabella & Associates
927 N. Northlake Way, Suite 108
Seattle, WA 98103, (206) 632-6272

Videotapes (continued)

Video Titles:

- *Alcohol and Boating? It's Your Choice.* Teenagers examine the consequences of alcohol and boating from their perspective.

- *It Could Have Been Prevented,* MAPV-18. Boating safety for small boats with emphasis on the dangers of alcohol and boating.

- *When Seconds Count: Care and Maintenance of Immersion Suits,* MAPV-38. Inspection, donning, maintenance, and storage of immersion suits.

Available from:

Alaska Marine Safety Education Association (AMSEA)
Box 2592
Sitka, AK 99835, (907) 747-3287
www.uaf.edu/seagrant/amsea/

Video Titles:

- *Hypothermia,* MAPV-1. Recognition and treatment of hypothermia.

- *Cold Water Near Drowning,* MAPV-2. Background and treatment of cold water near-drowning.

- *Sea Survival,* MAPV-3. Handling a sea survival emergency in a life raft with emphasis on the Seven Steps to Survival.

- *Shore Survival,* MAPV-4. Survival on shore with emphasis on the Seven Steps to Survival.

- *Frostbite and Other Cold Injuries,* MAPV-17. Recognition and treatment of frostbite and other cold injuries, but not hypothermia.

- *It Could Have Been Prevented,* MAPV-18. Boating safety for small boats with emphasis on the dangers of alcohol and boating.

- *When Seconds Count: Care and Maintenance of Immersion Suits,* MAPV-38. Inspection, donning, maintenance, and storage of immersion suits.

Available from:

Marine Advisory Program, University of Alaska
2221 E. Northern Lights Blvd. #110
Anchorage, AK 99508-4140, (907) 274-9691

Glossary

Aft: near, toward, or at the back (stern) of a boat.

Amidships: in or toward the part of a ship midway between front and back.

Bilge: the lowest point of a boat's inner hull; or the part of the underwater body of a boat between the flat of the bottom and the vertical sides.

Boom: a post projecting from the mast (pole) on a boat.

Bow: the forward part of a boat.

Bridge: the part of a boat's superstructure from which the boat is navigated.

Broach: to veer dangerously so as to lie broadside to the waves or wind.

Bulwarks: the sides of a boat above the upper deck.

Capsize: turn over.

Carabiner: an oblong metal ring with a hinged side, used to hold a freely running rope.

Chart: navigation map.

Cockpit: a space or compartment in a boat from which it is steered.

Deck: a platform in a boat forming the floor for its compartments.

Dinghy: a small boat used as a tender; or a small sailboat or a rubber life raft.

Downwind: in the direction the wind is blowing.

Following seas: seas moving in the direction the boat is heading.

Fore: in or near the front (bow) of a boat.

Flotation: material that floats, used to make other things float.

Flying bridge: highest navigational bridge on a boat.

Freeboard: the distance between the waterline and the main deck of a boat, or between waterline and the upper edge of the side of a small boat.

Galley: the kitchen on a boat.

Gunwale: the upper edge of a boat's side.

Hatch: a deck opening that provides access to the space below.

Hull: the frame or body of a boat exclusive of masts, sails, and rigging.

Inboard: inside a boat's hull; or a motor fitted inside the boat.

Keel: a fin-like projection extending from a boat's hull to control rolling.

Glossary

Knot: 1.15 mph.

Lanyard: a piece of rope or line for fastening something in a boat.

Leeward: situated away from the wind.

Lifeline: a rope used for saving or preserving life; or a line along the outer edge of the deck of a boat.

Line: a rope used on a boat.

Lookout: a person keeping watch.

Mast: a long pole rising from the keel or deck of a boat and supporting the booms and rigging.

Outboard: outside a boat's sides; or a propulsion motor attached at the transom.

Port: the left side of a boat looking forward.

Quartering seas: coming from a point in back of the beam of a ship but not directly astern.

Quoit: a flattened circle of rope for throwing.

Rigging: lines used aboard a boat especially in working sail and supporting masts and spars.

Rudder: a flat piece attached upright to the stern of a boat so that it can be turned, causing the vessel to turn in the same direction.

Shoreside: at or near a shore.

Skiff: a small boat.

Skipper: the master of a boat.

Starboard: the right side of a boat looking forward.

Stern: the rear end of a boat.

Swamp: fill with water.

Tender: a small boat used to transport people, gear, or supplies.

Transom: the planking that forms the stern of a square-ended boat.

Upwind: in the direction from which the wind is blowing.

Wake: the track left by a boat moving in water.

Watch: a time during which a person on a boat is on duty; the person on a boat required to be on duty during a particular watch; or a sailor's assigned duty period.

Wheel watch: the person steering the boat and looking out for hazards.

Wheelhouse: a deckhouse containing the steering wheel, compass, and navigating equipment.

Index